Pitt Latin American Series

THE MANIPULATION OF CONSENT

The State and Working-Class Consciousness in Brazil

YOUSSEF COHEN

UNIVERSITY OF PITTSBURGH PRESS

Published by the University of Pittsburgh Press, Pittsburgh, Pa., 15260

Feffer and Simons, Inc., London
Manufactured in the United States of America

Library of Congress Cataloging-in-Publication Data

Cohen, Youssef.
The manipulation of consent : the state and working-class consciousness in Brazil / Youssef Cohen.
p. cm. — (Pitt Latin American series)
Bibliography: p.
Includes index.
ISBN 0-8229-3829-4. — ISBN 0-8229-5806-6 (pbk.)
1. Labor and laboring classes—Brazil—Political activity. 2. Elite (Social sciences)—Brazil—History. 3. Labor policy—Brazil—History.
I. Title. II. Series
HD8286.5.C64 1989
305.5'62'0981—dc19 89-5403
CIP

To Vera de Souza Gouvea

Contents

Tables and Figures

TABLES

FIGURES

Acknowledgments

I am grateful to the Ford Foundation, which sponsored the survey used in this book, and to the Instituto Universitário de Pesquisas do Rio de Janeiro and the Center for Political Research, Institute for Social Research, University of Michigan, which jointly conducted that survey.

For their advice and criticism, I am deeply grateful to Peter Bachrach, Brian R. Brown, Philip E. Converse, Frederick W. Frey, Joanne Gowa, Charles E. Lindblom, Peter J. McDonough, James M. Malloy, Jack H. Nagel, A. F. K. Organski, Franco Pavoncello, Nelson do Valle Silva, Amaury de Souza and Peter A. Swenson.

To my wife, Lindsay M. Wright, I owe more than I could possibly express.

Philadelphia
May 1987

THE MANIPULATION OF CONSENT

Chapter 1

INTRODUCTION

IT BEGAN early on March 31, 1964. At dawn, General Mourão Filho marched his troops on Rio de Janeiro to depose President João Goulart. By the late morning of April 1, Mourão Filho had been joined by General Amaury Kruel, commander of the Second Army centered in São Paulo, and by General Âncora, commander of the First Army in Rio de Janeiro. On the night of April 1, Goulart fled to Pôrto Alegre, and the president of the Senate, Auro de Moura Andrade, declared the presidency vacant. Following constitutional procedure, the president of the Chamber of Deputies, Ranieri Mazilli, was sworn in as acting president of the Republic. The next day the entire Third Army joined the revolt, forcing Goulart to flee to the interior of Rio Grande do Sul. On the fourth day of April, Goulart took asylum in Uruguay. Thus ended the Brazilian democratic regime—in power since 1946—and a vicious military dictatorship began, which was to last for more than two decades.[1]

The military had met little resistance. Goulart and his retinue had grossly overestimated their political strength.[2] From the workers and the left, where it was most expected, resistance came only faintly. The leftist General Labor Command (CGT) called a general strike on March 30, but the workers did not respond. Cities barely slowed down on April 1, and the frantic appeals of Justice Minister Abelardo Jurema for the people to take to the streets had no effect whatsoever. Finally, when on

April 2, Brizola, one of the most popular politicians of his time, urged his fellow *gauchos* to take up arms against the military, nothing worthy of notice ever ensued. Brizola himself fled shortly thereafter to Uruguay, where he joined his brother-in-law, João Goulart.

The lack of working-class resistance to the military is usually attributed to the political divisions among the left and the labor leadership, to its disorganization, to Goulart's unwillingness to fight, and of course, to the fear of retaliation. These factors are certainly important, but they do not exhaust the range of possible explanatory variables. One other possibility is that the workers *favored* military intervention. This possibility should be seriously considered because, as I intend to show, the available data on the behavior, beliefs, and attitudes of Brazilian workers indicate that the majority of urban workers were in favor of the military. To be sure, there were active militant workers who were strongly opposed to the military. But, as we shall see, these militant workers were only a small minority even in urban centers, where support for Goulart was strongest.

In showing that there was a great deal of support for the military among the working class, I have no intention of disparaging Brazilian workers. I have no intention either of reviving Lipset's argument concerning working-class authoritarianism or of blaming the emergence of the military regime on the authoritarian values of Brazilian workers.[3] On the contrary, my purpose is to show that the authoritarian political beliefs and values that ultimately led workers to favor the military over Goulart were originally instilled in workers by Brazilian elites. What is more, it is also possible to show that the authoritarian elite ideology instilled in workers served the interests of elites far better than the interests of the working class. My main purpose is precisely to describe the insidious power mechanisms by which Brazilian elites shaped the beliefs and values of workers, preventing them from acquiring the democratic values that would have better served their interests. In doing so, I hope to reveal the means by which such insidious mechanisms employed in the service of authoritarianism can be counteracted.

STATE ELITES, WORKERS, AND ORGANIC STATISM

The authoritarian ideology that led workers to favor military intervention was first spread among them by the elite of intellectuals, politicians, and military officers who seized the state apparatus in 1930.[4] That state elite was able to impart much autonomy and power to the central state apparatus. It expanded and restructured the state in ways that gave it overwhelming power over society, and the elite later used this power to launch and sponsor capitalist industrialization in Brazil.[5] Among the state structures created by the state elite of the thirties was the corporative labor system, which was designed to defuse class conflict and promote collaboration between classes. These corporative institutions have since then enabled Brazilian elites to control the working class and secure its quiescence.

This effect of corporative institutions has been widely recognized.[6] Over and over again, students of the corporative labor system have shown how such a state structure secures the quiescence of workers through cooptation. Corporative organizations, however, do more than that. They not only coopt workers but also indoctrinate them. Through the corporative structures, the state elite of the thirties as well as later elites were able to gain the consent of the working class to a far greater extent than is usually believed. As I will show in this book, there is enough evidence to argue that, through the corporative structures created in the thirties and still in operation at the present time, Brazilian elites instilled in workers, and maintained among them, the beliefs and values of a frankly authoritarian ideology. By doing so, Brazilian elites prevented workers from acquiring beliefs and values conducive to political action directed at redressing the injustices of capitalist industrialization. State elites were thus able to secure at relatively low cost the quiescence of workers during the first four decades of industrialization.

The authoritarian ideology of Brazilian elites that workers eventually internalized gained much currency in the thirties, when liberalism was under attack on a worldwide scale. Because of its reliance on the state, rather than on the market, as the best principle of social organization, Bolivar Lamounier has dubbed it a "state ideology."[7] Like other authoritarian ideologies, this particular Brazilian one has its roots in the tradition of political thought Alfred Stepan refers to as the organic-statist conception of the state.[8] According to this view, the good polity is one in which the component parts of society are harmoniously integrated into an organic whole. In such a polity, a powerful state is assigned the role of achieving and preserving such an organic harmony. This strong and benevolent state interprets the common good and is empowered to structure society to achieve that good.

In its modern twentieth-century form, organic statism strikes a middle ground between the liberal-democratic and the totalitarian views of the state. From an economic point of view, it advocates a far more interventionist state than the liberal one, even in its Keynesian form, but it neither abolishes private property nor completely destroys market institutions.[9] The autonomy of the private economic sphere is preserved to a far greater extent than in socialist economic thought. Similarly, from a political point of view, although in principle organic statism is clearly averse to democratic institutions, it allows a greater degree of autonomous political participation by social groups than that allowed by either fascism or communism. Participation is to occur, of course, within the structures and limits established by the state. But the state in organic-statist ideology is barred from the total penetration of society characteristic of fascism and communism.[10] Whereas in fascist as well as in communist thought the state is conceived of as absolute, in organic statism the state is not to eliminate the spheres of private action. The individual, the family, and private associations are given an independent place in the organic whole as well as an important function in achieving the common good. Each of these functional parts is to be self-managing and is to participate in the achievement of the general welfare. The state is to shape the action of the constituent parts to the extent necessary to achieve a harmonious whole but is not to destroy or absorb their functions.

ORGANIC STATISM, STATE BUILDING, AND DELAYED INDUSTRIALIZATION

Organic-statist ideologies appealed to the Latin American elites who in the thirties greatly expanded the power of the state and led their countries into the industrial era for the same reasons that other illiberal ideologies appealed to the European elites who in the nineteenth century led their backward countries into modernity.[11] As Alexander Gershenkron once noted, the more backward nations of continental Europe had to make a relatively greater effort to initiate their industrialization.[12] If they were to industrialize rapidly, they had to borrow the most modern and efficient techniques of the advanced countries. This meant industrializing with larger plants and on a considerably larger scale. To do so, backward countries had to raise large amounts of capital on very short notice. In the acutely backward nations—as in Russia, for instance—this could be done only through the "compulsory machinery of government," that is, by heavily taxing the population.[13] Obviously, only illiberal ideologies could legitimize the strong state that was necessary to perform such a task and justify its increasing intervention in the economy that the progress of industrialization would inevitably require. Furthermore, illiberal ideologies could justify the great sacrifice the lower classes had to make in shouldering most of the burden of industrial growth. Praising the state as a benevolent entity that would protect and lead the people into the promised land made it easier for elites to exact a major toll from the lower classes and for those classes to accept their burden.

For all of these reasons, illiberal ideologies held much appeal for the elites who promoted the industrialization of backward nations. As Gershenkron reminds us, the men who promoted French industrialization under Napoleon III were ardent

Saint-Simonian socialists, and Saint-Simonism also had much influence in industrializing Germany.[14] The need for ideologies that were in fact secular religions was even more pronounced in Russia, where the "barriers of stagnation" were even sturdier. There, nothing less than orthodox Marxism could perform the function of motivating elites and masses to make the enormous effort to propel their country into the new industrial age.

Since the state performed a central role in the industrialization of Latin America, illiberal ideologies were also extremely appealing to the elites who led the region into the industrial age.[15] The Catholic and organic-statist background of those elites was averse, however, to both fascism and communism. They therefore sought a middle ground between those totalitarian ideologies, on the one hand, and liberal democracy, on the other. This is clearly the case for the Brazilian elite of the thirties. Guided by the state ideology, this elite inaugurated an authoritarian-corporative regime with the intent of promoting collaboration between social classes.[16] In a deliberate attempt to prevent the class conflicts of laissez-faire industrialization, they created corporative institutions that they believed would promote harmony between classes. They thought that in this way the state would ensure that all social groups benefited from industrialization and further the social harmony envisioned by organic statism.

The Brazilian state elite had the full support of the business elites. In Brazil, as in many countries that had a relatively late industrialization, business elites were highly dependent on the protection of the state.[17] They had to rely on the state for a steady supply of capital, for protection from foreign competition, and also to secure the quiescence of the working class. To this vulnerable bourgeoisie, the organic statism of the Brazilian state ideology was therefore extremely appealing.[18] The business elite thus joined the state elite in extolling the virtues of the authoritarian-corporative regime of the late thirties—hoping, among other things, that it would promote collaboration on the part of the working class.

Brazilian elites got more than they had bargained for. Not

only were workers relatively quiescent for at least the first four decades of industrialization. As I will show, most workers also internalized the basic tenets of the authoritarian state ideology. During the democratic period (1946–1964) that followed the end of the authoritarian-corporative regime (1937–1945), they continued to hold such authoritarian beliefs, even though these were clearly against their best interests. The task of this book is to show this and to explain how Brazilian state elites and the corporative state structures they created diffused and maintained the organic-statist state ideology among the working class.

THEORETICAL RELEVANCE

The State as an Actor

The main argument of this book runs counter to "society-centered" explanations of patterns of working-class formation and of class conflict, that is, it questions the explanations of these patterns that are based mainly on social and economic factors. For a long time now, patterns of working-class organization, action, and consciousness have been seen mainly as a function of the characteristics of the process of capitalist industrialization.[19] The effect of the action of state elites and state structures was largely neglected. This neglect is now being redressed by some social scientists, who have convincingly argued that the patterns of working-class formation and the structure of class conflicts are far from being exclusively the result of the characteristics of capitalist industrialization. Rather, the considerable variations in the patterns of working-class formation are largely due to the actions of state elites and state structures.

One of the best examples of recent work directed at showing the impact of the state on class is that of Ira Katznelson.[20] Katznelson has criticized society-centered studies of working-class formation for assuming that organized class-conscious working classes naturally emerge from the process of capitalist industrialization. He has argued that if we look at real working classes rather than at the "theoretically constructed proletariats" of society-centered approaches, we shall find far more variation in the patterns of working-class formation than is usually assumed. These differences can be accounted for only by a state-centered explanation. To show this, Katznelson compared the patterns of working-class formation of the United States and England. His work as well as that of Martin Shefter show that the relatively low level of political capacity and power of the American industrial working class is due to state-centered factors.[21] They show that factors such as the timing of democratization in relation to capitalist industrialization, the growth of the national state, and the legal conditions under which working-class organizations had to operate greatly affected working-class action, organization, and consciousness. Similarly, I argue in this book that the political consciousness of Brazilian workers was shaped by state elites and state structures rather than by workers' direct experience of the process of capitalist industrialization.

This renewed interest in the role of the state in the study of class and class conflict is part of a broader movement that has brought the state back into the social sciences.[22] From the fifties to the mid-seventies, mainstream sociology and political science saw the state as a mere reflection of civil society rather than as an actor in its own right. The state was seen as a neutral mechanism that allocates values according to the pressures of autonomously formed groups competing with each other to maximize their own self-defined interests. Public officials were conceived of as referees that ensure the game is fairly played, and public policies as the outcome of political competition. In such a view, there is, of course, no room for a view of the state as an independent actor that shapes and even restructures its own society.

The same is true of Marxist theory. Orthodox Marxism with its views of the state as a mere instrument of class rule obviously has no room for the state as an autonomous actor. But even more recent neo-Marxist formulations, which see the state either as an arena for political class struggles or as an entity that functions to secure the reproduction of capitalist relations of production and ensures capital accumulation, still see the state as ultimately shaped by the mode of production and by class struggle.[23] Even these neo-Marxist formulations rule out the possibility that the state itself may shape or even transform the mode of production and class struggles. As Theda Skocpol has noted, they rule out crucial forms of state action and therefore still fail to see the state as an actor in its own right.[24]

Since the mid-seventies, this has changed. Social scientists have increasingly focused on the state as an object of investigation. A wide range of phenomena have been studied in relation to the impact of state elites, state policies, and state structures.[25] These studies show that we can no longer see states as a mere reflection of society or the economy. They strongly suggest that the state should be viewed not only as structured by civil society but also as structuring it. Alfred Stepan captured this view of the state when he argued for a conceptualization of the state as "the continuous administrative, legal, bureaucrtic and coercive systems that attempt not only to structure relations *between* civil society and public authority in a polity but also to structure many crucial relations *within* civil society as well."[26] This conception of the state allows for the possibility of independent state action without postulating that the state always behaves as such. The important question is not, as Stepan puts it, whether states structure relations between public authority and society and within society itself but "the degree to which, and the means through which, they do so."[27] States also vary in terms of the degree to which the strategic elite in charge of its apparatus is cohesive, that is, in the extent to which the state can be considered as one single actor; they differ as to whether they are procedurally neutral and autonomous as opposed to being a class instrument or the instrument of foreign groups; and they vary in terms of the degree to which they achieve obedience through force or through what Antonio Gramsci called ideological hegemony.

The Brazilian state elite of the thirties is clearly an instance of a cohesive elite that restructured the relations between state and society as well as crucial relations within civil society. As we shall see, the state structures they created not only shaped the relations between social classes but also came very close to achieving ideological hegemony, especially with respect to the working class.

The Power Analytic Framework

At a more general level, this book explores the general proposition that the beliefs and values of socially deprived groups are largely a function of the power relations in which they are involved. This is to say that the beliefs and values of the underprivileged result from the exercise of power by elites rather than being generated by the underprivileged themselves. If it is true that Brazilian state elites shaped the values of workers through corporative state structures, then the Brazilian case would be a concrete instance in favor of the general proposition above involving the connection between power and the political consciousness of the underprivileged. The concept of power thus stands at the center of this study, which is mainly concerned with showing that the authoritarian beliefs of Brazilian workers are an outcome of their power relations with state elites.

By applying the concept of power to the study of Brazilian workers, I hope to show more generally that the study of state-society relations would stand to benefit a great deal from an explicit recognition of the fact that the concept of power stands at the heart of its object of investigation. The conceptual apparatus built around the concept of power—the "power analytic framework," if you will—can be of much help in the systematic empirical investigation not only of the relation between state power and political consciousness but of state-society relations in general. Conversely, the empirical investigation of the concrete mechanisms involved by which state power is exercised can add to the still largely imperfect theoretical knowledge of the operation of power. I hope to show in this book how the state-society approach and a power analytic framework can be integrated in order to enhance each other.

As a final word, I should add that the customary section on

the plan of the book, which usually appears at the end of the introductory chapter, has been moved to the end of the next chapter. Since the structure of this book emerges more naturally from the following chapter, it is best to lay it out there rather than here.

Chapter 2

POWER AND POLITICAL CONSCIOUSNESS

THE LANGUAGE of the state-society approach cannot rid itself of the notion of power. To say that state elites, the state structures they fashion, and the policies they implement *shape* relations within civil society is to say that state elites *exercise power* over social actors to produce such outcomes in civil society. To say that Brazilian state elites and the corporative state structures they created shaped the political consciousness of workers is to say that they exercised power over workers in order to instill in them the authoritarian-corporative beliefs and values of the state ideology. Though such statements on power relations seem simple enough, there is more to them than meets the eye. The concept of power is treacherous, and the empirical study of power relations is difficult. To see what state-society statements such as the particular one concerning the shaping of the consciousness of Brazilian workers entail and how they can be empirically verified, it is therefore necessary to discuss at some length the concept of power and the power analytic framework. This is what I will do in this chapter.

THE POWER RELATION

Power is a relation, not a property. Although many people think of power as a property, as something one *has,* such a conception of power is misleading. To say that Rockefeller had power in the same way that he had money, for instance, is misleading in more than one way. First of all, the statement does not specify exactly over whom Rockefeller had power. It thus gives the impression that Rockefeller had the upper hand in every situation, when in fact he was often far from getting what he wanted. Second, the statement suggests that Rockefeller had power *because* he had money. This is also misleading, because it involves an inference about power itself from what is merely a power *resource,* namely, money.[1] And such inferences are unwarranted. For money, guns, or any other power resource do not automatically confer power; whether they do or do not depends on the particular situation. In some situations, money and guns are virtually useless; intelligence, good looks, or athletic skills, for instance, sometimes carry the day.[2] Thus, in order to avoid mistaken inferences we must define power as a relation and specify not only who has power but also over whom he has it, with respect to what, and under what circumstances. I shall therefore use here the concept of power as a relation.

To be more specific, I shall define power, after Frederick Frey, as "a relation between actors such that the behavior of one actor at least partly causes the behavior of another," where actors can be either individuals or groups.[3] There are three basic elements to this definition. In the first place, the power relation is a relation between human beings. Second, it is a causal relation. And, third, both the causing entity and the entity caused are, of all characteristics of human beings, behaviors. The first two elements are much less controversial than the third. Let us consider each of them in turn.

Most social scientists agree that the concept of power should be restricted to relations between human beings.[4] The term *power* is often used to refer to the capacity human beings have to change nature, or, conversely, to that of nature to change human beings. This is the usage found in statements such as "a tornado has the power to lift a house from the ground," and "human beings have the power to erect cities." Although this is a common usage, social scientists have preferred to restrict the concept to relations between humans, because causal relations between sentient beings are of a very different nature than those involving other entities. Phenomena such as learning and motivation are an integral part of causal relations between humans, whereas they are absent from those involving other entities. I shall therefore follow the dominant usage of power as a relation between human beings.

The approach to power as a type of causation is now a dominant one. It has become so through the work of Herbert Simon, James March, and Robert Dahl.[5] As Jack Nagel noted, there are at least three reasons for the popularity of such an approach.[6] First, there are intuitive similarities between causal relations and power relations. Intuitively, the word *influence* is almost a synonym for *cause* and *power*, and both causal and power relations are assymetric. In the second place, causal conceptions of power force us to state the connection between resources and power as an empirical hypothesis, which prevents tautological statements concerning power relations. Instead of tautologically saying that the military have power because they have weapons, for instance, the causal approach would force us to ask whether their weapons do in fact cause the behavior they may have wanted to occur. Finally, the concept of power as a causal relation enables researchers to use a variety of methods and techniques employed in empirical research, from canons of theory construction to statistical measures.

There are problems with the notion of causality, of course. After Hume's attack on the concept of causality, many have objected to its use. Since these objections are dealt with extensively elsewhere, I shall not deal with them here.[7] Suffice it to say that the problems of causality are not insurmountable and that, anyhow, scientists are unable to work without the idea of cause. In any event, because of the work of Herbert Simon and others we now have the means to deal with the notion of causality in a way that takes into consideration Hume's critique.[8]

As for the third element of the definition of power used here—*behavior* both as the causing and caused entities—there is significant disagreement among social scientists. The main objection to a definition of power in terms of an influential behavior, that is, in terms of the behavior of the influencer as a cause, is that the term *behavior* refers to overt physical movements, or acts, and therefore excludes an important type of power relation. As Nagel has remarked, a definition of power in terms of influential behavior excludes the type of power known as *anticipated reactions,* because it is a relation in which the influencer does not exhibit any behavior, in the sense that he does not act. In the case of anticipated reactions, the influencee anticipates what the influencer wants and behaves accordingly.[9] No action is required on the part of the influencer. For example, we often do what our bosses or spouses want us to do without them having to ask or command it. Since we do so because we anticipate their preferences, Nagel suggested that we use the *preferences* rather than the behavior of the influencer as the causing factor in the power relation.[10]

As Frey has argued, however, there is no need whatsoever to dispose of the notion of infuential behavior in order to solve the problem of anticipated reactions. On the contrary, we need that notion, since "preferences are known only through behavior (acts)."[11] The influencer must convey his preferences, if any, so that the influencee can anticipate them. The young lawyer who, without being asked, wears a dark suit to please his seniors does not merely imagine that this is what his seniors want him to do. The influential behavior in this case may be simply the wearing of dark suits by the influential seniors. Even if unaware of doing so, the influencer must engage in some kind of influential behavior for us to consider a case of anticipated reaction as an instance of a power relation. Otherwise we would have to include cases where the anticipation by the influencee is completely autonomous, which would disqualify his behavior as being caused by an exercise of power. The case of someone who attempts to assassinate a president because he thinks the woman of his dreams wants him to do so is a case of anticipated reactions that may or may not involve power. If we have reason to believe that the woman in question did influence the would-be assassin, then his behavior would in fact be an outcome of a power relation. On the other hand, if the would-be assassin is a lunatic who unjustifiably imagined the woman's wishes, we certainly would not count this case of anticipated reactions as an instance of power. And to decide the matter, we would need some evidence on the woman's *behavior.* We would have to know her preferences, which we can know only through her behavior, and whether she engaged in any behavior that could have influenced the would-be assassin.

There are two types of anticipated reactions. One involves power and may properly be called an anticipated reaction. The other does not involve power and should be referred to as *autonomous anticipation.*[12] In the latter case, an actor's anticipation of another actor's behavior is the product of his imagination. "The other actor may not even exist, as when children avoid the mean old man who lives in the (actually empty) haunted house or, possibly, nations react to an 'international communist bloc' that may be a mere chimera."[13] Whether or not we can determine if a particular case of anticipation is a case of autonomous anticipation or actually involves power will depend on whether or not we can establish that there was an influential behavior on the part of a possible influencer.

That some overt form of behavior is necessary to establish whether power is involved or not, and that therefore power should be defined in terms of behavior rather than preferences, does not entirely settle the matter, however. The notion of influential behavior as a causal factor excludes some subtle and elusive cases, such as that presented by Nagel about "parents who teach their son to obey the law in the presence of a policeman, and the youth is law-abiding in those circumstances but not in others."[14] Most analysts, including Nagel, would agree that in this case the policeman had power over the youth. If this is the case, one could then argue that the behavioral conception of power should be rejected, because it excludes the case of the policeman having power merely by being there; he did not behave, in the sense of "doing" something. Yet such an objection to the notion of influential behavior is based on too narrow a conception of behavior. There is no reason to restrict the use of the term in such a way. A broader conception of behavior "includes presence in a specific spatio-temporal location as behavior."[15] The mere presence of the policeman, or a teacher, or a parent, constitutes influential behavior in that it can clearly affect the behavior of a child. In this broader sense, behavior includes feeling, thinking, or even sitting still or sleeping.[16] Since it seems that we cannot do without some notion of behavior, it would seem advisable to use it in this broader sense.

To conclude then, I shall here define power as Frey has, that is, as a relation in which one actor's behavior causes (or alters) the behavior of another. Actors can be either individuals or groups, and behavior is used in the broader sense of the term. The elements of a power relation are therefore the *influencer,* who causes the behavior of the *influencee,* the *influential behavior* of the influencer, the *response* of the influencee, and the *setting* in which the relation occurs.[17] In the Brazilian case studied in this book, the Brazilian state elite is the influencer; the workers, the influencee; the creation of corporative institutions, the influential behavior; and the internalization of authoritarian beliefs and values by workers, the response. The setting is given by the particular context of Brazilian politics from the thirties to the sixties. My task is to show how by creating and maintaining corporative institutions the Brazilian political elites of that period were able to instill into Brazilian workers their authoritarian ideology.

POWER AND CONFLICT

Exerting power is often thought of as forcing some actor to do what he does not want to do. Power is thus associated with conflict, resistance, and force.[18] According to the definition of power used in this book, however, power can be exercised in the complete absence of conflict.[19] All that is required is that the influential behavior of the influencer cause the behavior of the influencee. Just as real power often occurs in the absence of conflict, this definition does not require conflict. Power is allowed to occur without any resistance from the influencee, as it often does in real life. For example, a father can persuade his daughter to put a down payment on a slightly bigger house than she would have otherwise bought without having to coerce his prudent offspring. A wife can gently lead her husband to buy a dark suit rather than a bright one, and have him thank her for the suggestion. In these cases, the influencee has to choose among alternatives that are attractive to him. The influencer merely induces him to choose among several attractive alternatives.[20] He certainly exerts power, but there is no resistance on the part of the influencee. Their power relation is free from conflict.

If the examples above are trivial, there are others that are not. Instances of indoctrination are clearly important examples of power without conflict. In the case of indoctrination, power is exerted not only without any resistance from the influencee but also without his awareness. It is thus the most effective form of power. Yet, if we assume that whenever people choose to behave in certain ways without being forced to do so no power is being exercised over them, we deny even the possibility of indoctrination. By doing so we would dismiss offhand what may be a widespread phenomenon. We would be saying that in the absence of coercion, resistance, and conflict, people choose their own beliefs, values, and behavior. Yet there is enough evidence at least to suspect that elites shape the beliefs and values of the masses without resorting to force in a variety of very different societies. This is also true of Western capitalist democracies. For a very long time now, many observers and analysts have pointed out that the elites of Western democracies use their resources to control the processes of communication and socialization in order to disseminate values among the underprivileged and the powerless that can secure their conformity and quiescence. In this way they can gain control over the lower classes without resorting to force, simply by preventing the very emergence of disagreement and conflict.[21] Whether this is in fact true or merely imaginative babble is still largely unknown. But it surely is a plausible hypothesis. Yet mainstream political scientists have not been giving it much attention.

As Charles Lindblom, a mainstream political scientist himself, has recently noticed, such scientists tend to assume that the process of socialization is largely a beneficial one. Lindblom has criticized them for overlooking the possibility that the "process they study, whether called socialization or indoctrination, is an instrument through which the advantaged, with their advantages in the control of communications, teach the disadvantaged to accept their disadvantages."[22] Underlying the bias of these mainstream scientists is the assumption that the democratic process is benign in that it ultimately allows people to choose freely among alternative courses of action. Thus if people adhere to the norms of such democratic societies it is because they choose to do so, not because power has been exercised to lead them in that direction. In other words, it is assumed that if they are not forced to adhere to those norms, and such norms are followed in the absence of social conflict, power is not involved. No conflict, no power. Therefore indoctrination, which is power in the absence of conflict, is not considered as a genuine possibility in democratic societies.

That there is no observable conflict between the actors in a power relation does not mean, however, that they have the same interests. Obviously, if people can be indoctrinated, there is reason to suppose that the doctrine may be against their best interest. In this case, we would have an instance of power without conflict but with an opposition of interests.[23] But this should not lead one to infer that power will always be exercised in the presence of an opposition of interest, even when indoctrination is involved. An actor may persuade another actor to act in a way that is in the interest of this other actor, as in the case of a daughter who persuades her aging mother to invest her money in a more profitable way. In this case, the daughter would have influenced her mother in the absence of both conflict and an opposition of interest.

Since neither conflict nor an opposition of interests is built into our definition of power, it allows us to deal with all possible combinations of both elements. This flexibility of the definition is particularly useful in analyzing the Brazilian case. The Brazilian case, as we saw, is an instance of a power relation in the form of indoctrination, that is, it is an instance of power in the absence of conflict. The political elite indoctrinated workers with an authoritarian ideology. But, as I will show, such an ideology was against the interests of Brazilian workers. Thus, the Brazilian case is an instance of power without conflict yet with an opposition of interests. By indoctrinating workers with authoritarian values, Brazilian elites both prevented conflict and promoted their own interests at the expense of those of workers.

That Brazilian elites promoted their own interests over those of workers does not mean that they meant to do so. Although state elites had as their explicit goal the prevention of class conflict and the harmonization of class interests, it is not clear whether they genuinely believed that there was no fundamental opposition of interests, or were perversely manipulating the working class. This takes us to the next problem in the analysis of power, the problem of intentionality.

POWER AND INTENTION

To many of us it seems absurd to say that someone exerted power over another person when that other person ends up behaving in ways the first person had not intended.[24] "Power," says Dennis Wrong, "is identical with *intended* and effective influence."[25] Although most analysts probably would agree with Wrong in requiring that intention be incorporated in a definition of power, there are good reasons not to do so.

Nagel, for instance, contends that intention should not be used as the causal factor in a power relation because this would exclude one of the most important instances of a power relation: anticipated reactions.[26] In such a case, as we saw, the influencee does what he believes are the influencer's wishes without any attempt by the influencer to influence him. Since the influencer has no apparent intention of exerting influence, and this case of anticipated reactions is generally considered to be an instance of a power relation, it follows that intention is not a necessary aspect of power.

Another objection is raised by Frey, who argues that intention should not be built into a definition of power because its inclusion would force us to exclude "both non-intended and anti-intended causal relations among actors."[27] To Frey, this would be unfortunate, because not only are nonintended and antiintended relations extremely important in their own right, they are often intimately associated in important ways with intended relations. For instance, by excluding antiintended relations, we would be excluding from our definition of power the well-known and frequent power relation usually referred to as the kiss of death. In such a relation, the influencer jeopardizes his protegé by attempting to use his influence to protect him or do him a favor. Another common power relation that would be excluded is one in which the influencer unintendedly produces unwanted effects on the influencee or on other actors by producing intended effects on him. In all of these cases, the unintended results are in fact produced by the influential behavior of the influencer, who therefore has the *power* to produce them.

Nagel's and Frey's objections to the incorporation of intention into the very definition of power override the main arguments in favor of such an incorporation.

One such argument, put forth by Geoffrey Debnam, is that Nagel and others define intention in a way that forces us to reject its inclusion in the concept of power.[28] Debnam argues that if intention is seen as rational consciousness involving deliberate and calculated behavior, then it cannot be included in the concept of power without at the same time excluding important types of power relations. However, if, after Merton, one defines the aim of action as nebulous, hazy, and semiconscious, then intentions can be incorporated in a definition of power that would not be too excluding. But this is clearly not the case, for even if such a redefinition of intention allows us to deal with instances of anticipated reactions as instances of power, it certainly cannot handle non-intended and anti-intended relations of power.

Another main argument in favor of the inclusion of intention is that, unless it is included, we would be unable to distinguish between power and other forms of causal relations.[29] This is allegedly the case because intention is necessary in order to distinguish causal relations between sentient beings from those between insentient beings. But there is no reason to do so. All we have to do is build the notion of actors into the concept of power and define them as sentient beings, as we already did.

Finally, there are those who, like Wrong, argue that we should not count unintended relations as power relations because that would equate social interaction with power.[30] They argue that if interaction equals power, then the study of power becomes the study of all human behavior. It would subsume all the social sciences, which would be undesirable to most social scientists. This argument, however, is based on a misunderstanding of both the concept of social interaction and that of power. For power is indeed an aspect of all social interaction, and one can study any human interaction from a power perspective. But it is not the only aspect. One can study social interaction not only from a power perspective but also from an economic perspective, from a communication perspective, from an affective perspective, and so on: "Interaction refers to the totality of aspects of human interchange, of which power is only one."[31] Thus it is not necessary to incorporate the notion of intention into the definition of power to distinguish between power and interaction.

It would seem, then, that we only lose by building intentionality into power. That is why I have chosen a definition that does not incorporate intentionality. Our definition requires one only to establish a causal link between the influential behavior and the response; there is no need to demonstrate that the influencer intended to produce the response through his influential behavior. This is particularly useful to the analysis of our case, for it is almost impossible to show that the Brazilian elites intended to indoctrinate workers by erecting corporative institutions. They certainly intended to prevent class conflict by building corporative institutions, and corporative institutions they did build. As Getúlio Vargas, the leader of the corporative state himself, put it in a speech to the Constituent Assembly in 1933, the corporative unions were "for the collaboration of labor and capital with the government."[32] But whether or not he and his followers thought of corporative institutions as major instruments of indoctrination is hard to establish.

In the last three chapters of this book I shall argue that Brazilian elites indoctrinated workers with the help of corporative institutions. I cannot be sure, however, that Brazilian elites saw, as I do, the link between corporative institutions and indoctrination nor that they intended to use such institutions to indoctrinate workers. Perhaps some of them did have a glimpse of the indoctrinating functions of the corporative state. Oliveira Vianna, for example, one of the major architects of the corporative state, saw the corporative associations as leading citizens "to identify with the state."[33] But it is more likely that most of the members of the state elite did not see this connection and therefore could not have intended to indoctrinate workers through corporative institutions. Whether this is or is not the case, however, cannot be easily established. But, as I have argued, there is no need to show that Brazilian elites intended to indoctrinate workers in order to establish that they did so. It is only necessary to show that the influential behavior of Brazilian elites—the creation of corporative institutions—was a major cause of the internalization of authoritarian beliefs and values by Brazilian workers.

THE EMPIRICAL STUDY OF POWER

An empirical identification of an exercise of power involves showing that the behavior of actor *B*, whom we think was influenced, was in fact caused by another actor, *A*, rather than being actor *B*'s autonomous decision. One has to show that if *A* had not influenced *B*, *B* would have behaved differently. As Steven Lukes puts it, "any attribution of the exercise of power . . . always implies a relevant counterfactual, to the effect that (but for *A*, or but for *A* together with any other sufficient conditions) *B* would otherwise have done, let us say, *b*" (rather than *a*, what *A* causes).[34] If we are to show then that *B* did *a* because of *A*'s behavior, we must be ready to offer empirical support for an assertion of the implied relevant counterfactual.

This is easy to do when there is an observable conflict between *A* and *B*. For, as Lukes remarks, "conflict provides the relevant counterfactual, so to speak, ready made."[35] If *B* wants *b*, and *A* wants *a*, and *A* prevails, we can safely infer that if *A* had not exercised power, *B* would have behaved differently. In the absence of conflict, however, how can we say that *A* causes *B*'s behavior? How can we assert the counterfactual (that were it not for *A*, *B* would have behaved differently) if *B* never manifests any wish to behave differently? These are the problems we must face here, since the main purpose of this book is to show that Brazilian workers were indoctrinated, and indoctrination is an instance of power without conflict. How can we show that, if it were not for Brazilian elites, workers would have different values and beliefs? How can we show that Brazilian workers would have had the same beliefs and values without any intervention on the part of political elites? In other words, how can we provide support for an assertion of the relevant counterfactual in this case of power without conflict?

Frey has provided a way of dealing with this problem.[36] He has offered a method that allows us to assess the plausibility of the relevant counterfactual in situations where there is reason to suppose that power has been exercised without conflict. He argued that in such cases we need to justify our expectation that, if it were not for *A*, *B* would have behaved differently, even though *B* never manifested any desire to do so. Once we have justified our expectations that *B* should have acted differently, we must also specify the influential behavior, or the *power mechanism*, by which *A* causes *B*'s behavior and prevents him from acting in the ways he should have according to our expectations. Thus, in our particular case of indoctrination, it is necessary to justify why one should expect Brazilian workers to hold different beliefs and values than those they have, and to describe the power mechanism by which Brazilian state elites indoctrinated them.

There are several ways of developing expectations about the political beliefs of *B*, the actor we believe would have acted differently had it not been for *A*'s exercise of power. One of them is theory. Although our theoretical knowledge about how people come to hold beliefs is far from perfect, we can certainly use available theories on the formation and change of attitudes and beliefs to develop expectations about those of a group—in our case, Brazilian workers. Of particular interest to this book are hypotheses concerning the development of group consciousness, especially where the reciprocal connection between participation and political consciousness is concerned. As we shall see, existing knowledge, though admittedly rudimentary, leads one to believe that Brazilian workers would have been more active and politically knowledgeable and would probably have held different views had working-class organizations been different. There is thus some theoretical reason to suspect a power mechanism at work preventing workers from holding certain political views.

A second tool for developing expectations is empirical comparison.[37] If, for example, in nine out of ten racist communities blacks engage in protest, one would suspect that some power mechanism is at work in the tenth community to prevent blacks from engaging in protest. Similarly, if, under similar circumstances, workers from other countries held beliefs that were more conducive to improving their situation than those held by Brazilian workers, one would suspect that some power mechanism is at work in Brazil to prevent workers from holding beliefs that would further their interests better than those they hold.

A third way of determining expectations concerning the behavior of a group, and one that would certainly make us expect Brazilian workers to act and think differently than they do, is to investigate the extent to which that group suffers from inequalities in the distribution of social rewards, such as wealth and prestige. If the group in question is extremely deprived, as Brazilian workers are, and if their political beliefs clearly prevent them from acting to improve their situation, as those of Brazilian workers do, it can then be concluded that there is good reason to suspect that power was exercised to induce the group to hold such paralyzing beliefs.

Even if we use the three methods above to argue that one should expect Brazilian workers to hold beliefs radically different from those they actually hold, and that we therefore suspect that the political elite have prevented them from holding the views they should hold, one must still show *how* exactly the elite prevented workers from holding those views. This step is required as a protection against the real possibility that the method used to develop our expectations has misled us to expect Brazilian workers to hold different views from those they do hold. Should this be the case, we would be unable to find a preventive mechanism, that is, the mechanism by which the Brazilian political elite prevented workers from holding the beliefs one would expect them to hold. Looking for the power mechanism is thus an essential check against the real possibility that the analyst may have developed wrong expectations.[38]

As I have already said, I shall argue that the power mechanism by which state elites indoctrinated Brazilian workers was built into the corporative institutions elites created during the dictatorship of the Estado Novo and maintained almost intact during the subsequent two decades of Brazilian democracy. This argument will be developed in chapters 5 and 6.

Before I specify the power mechanism, however, I shall first describe the authoritarian ideology the Brazilian political elite disseminated among workers and show how in fact Brazilian workers held beliefs and values highly congruent with that ideology. This will be done in chapter 3. In chapter 4, I will then justify my expectation that Brazilian workers would have held different beliefs and values had it not been for the influential behavior of political elites.

The description of the beliefs and values of Brazilian workers in the next chapter is based on extensive interviews, conducted between 1972 and 1973, of 617 urban workers. These interviews are part of a broader mass-elite political survey conducted in six Brazilian southeastern states. The mass sample, from which the interviews with urban workers were extracted, was a multistaged area probability sample (N = 1,314) of the adult population of six states: São Paulo, Rio de Janeiro, Guanabara, Minas Gerais, Rio Grande do Sul, and Espírito Santo.[39]

Chapter 3

THE STATE IDEOLOGY

When we interviewed them in the early seventies, Brazilian urban workers held political views that were astonishingly congruent with the authoritarian character of the military regime of 1964.[1] The congruence was so great as to lead one to believe that, in less than a decade, the military erased all trace of democratic values that may have been formed during the two decades of democracy that preceded the military coup.[2] But the evidence suggests otherwise. While the military may have reinforced the views of workers, it seems that they did not convert most workers into staunch authoritarians. There is good reason to believe that the views of workers had been of an authoritarian nature even before the installation of a military regime.

In this chapter I will argue that Brazilian workers have continuously held authoritarian-corporative beliefs since the Estado Novo, Vargas's corporative state. I will begin by describing briefly the Brazilian corporative state and the authoritarian ideology undergirding it. I will then show how the political views of workers were congruent with such an ideology both when we interviewed them, under the military regime, and before, under the democratic one.

THE ESTADO NOVO: THE BRAZILIAN CORPORATIVE STATE

In November of 1937 Getúlio Vargas assumed dictatorial powers through a military coup. During the resulting authoritarian regime, the Estado Novo (1937–45), Vargas erected an institutional network that was clearly meant to approximate an organic-statist model of governance.[3] As we saw, according to this model the state has the role of guiding, shaping, and supervising civil society. Its major function is to see that the major groups of society have harmonious rather than conflictive relations, and that society remains a functionally integrated organic whole. As society's guide and guardian, the state in the organic-statist model is to intervene in the economy to a far greater extent than in the classical liberal model in order to avoid the allegedly disruptive consequences of market competition. But it is not to stifle society, as does the state in the socialist model of governance. The organic-statist model accords an important role to the participation of private groups, though it does so within limits. The state determines those limits by shaping the institutional arrangement within which groups participate so as to promote harmony among them.

Since 1930 Vargas had been attempting to construct a powerful state along the lines prescribed by the organic-statist model. Such a task involved curbing the power of state governments, which formed a loose federation controlled by the major rural oligarchies.[4] By 1937 Vargas had already largely succeeded in increasing the power of the central government at the expense of the states and rural oligarchs. During the Estado Novo, this process was greatly accelerated. Toward the end of his dictatorship, Vargas had given the upper hand to the federal government where the most important policy decisions were concerned.[5]

Shortly after the beginning of World War II, Vargas further expanded the size, scope, and power of the central government by explicitly endorsing a policy of state-promoted industrialization.[6] The crash of 1929 had led to a more or less spontaneous and unintended spurt of import-substituting industrialization. The government had intervened to protect coffee growers from a disastrous fall in coffee prices and in the process of doing so had unintendedly promoted industrial growth.[7] This unintended incipient growth was later furthered by the deliberate policy of state intervention of the Estado Novo. The Depression and the war had convinced the political elite and the military that Brazil had to undergo rapid industrialization if it were to have a chance to become a powerful modern nation.[8] Vargas used the opportunity afforded by the war effort to expand the size and scope of the federal bureaucracy to promote industrialization both through indirect and direct mechanisms. A plethora of financial institutions, planning agencies, advisory bodies, technical groups, institutes, and corporations were created for this purpose.[9] Through this greatly expanded bureaucracy, the state, on the one hand, provided indirect incentives to industry such as tax incentives, import quotas, favorable exchange rates, generous credit, and wage controls, and, on the other hand, invested directly in infrastructural services and formed mixed and public enterprises in basic industries, such as steel and oil.[10] By the end of the Estado Novo, Vargas had erected an all-powerful state that had a predominant role in shaping economic policy and the course of the Brazilian economy. Both the organization of the state and the strong interventionist character it had acquired under Vargas outlasted him and the Estado Novo. The same is true of the corporative system created by Vargas to link the state to the private groups and interests of society.

Explicitly meant to harmonize the interests of capital and labor, the corporative system of interest representation was gradually built since 1930.[11] It took its full-blown form and was fully codified in law during the Estado Novo. The corporative system was designed to give the state a mediating function between employers and workers. It was hoped that by mediating the relations between these two groups, the state would transform potentially conflictive industrial relations into cooperative ones. In this way, it was thought, the class conflict that usually accompanied capitalist industrialization under the liberal state could be averted or at least minimized. Through corporative institutions, the Brazilian state could thus achieve its organic ideal of harmoniously integrating the major functional groups of society.

The corporative system consists of two parallel and symmetric hierarchies subordinated to the Ministry of Labor, one of employers' associations, the other of workers' unions. In the case of the official labor hierarchy, the lower level consists of the *sindicato*, the corporative union, which is given by the state exclusive representation of a predefined occupational category within an area roughly comparable to a county or township. The *sindicato* is then linked to the state federations, which are in turn linked to seven national confederations directly subordinated to the Ministry of Labor. Essentially the same three-level hierarchy is replicated in the case of the official organizations for employers.

In theory, the official corporative hierarchies have two functions. First, through their powerful mechanisms of control, the state can exact conformity to whatever it deems in the public interest. Second, through them the particular interests of social groups are supposed to find their expression: instead of clashing directly, employers and workers make their demands to the state through their corporative hierarchies. The state then manages potential conflicts, reconciling these particular demands to the public interest. It is thus the interplay between the functions of control and representation of corporative institutions that allows the organic state to subordinate particular private interests to the public interest without stifling them. Such an operation requires, however, that interest groups retain considerable autonomy in the management of their affairs. Otherwise the powerful controls of the corporative system would destroy the ability of these groups to represent themselves. If in theory this should not happen, in reality it does.

As one would expect, the symmetry between the two official hierarchies is only formal. There is no symmetry where the power relations between the state and the interest groups are concerned. Whereas employers have the resources to counteract the powerful controls built within the corporative framework, workers do not. Workers have no alternative but to attempt to influence the state through the official unions, and their resources are too meager to overcome the strong control mechanisms built by the state into their corporative organizations. Thus, although the organic-statist ideal postulates a considerable degree of autonomy for the functional groups, in practice it tends to stifle such autonomy for the subordinate class. Instead of integrating the major social groups into a harmonious whole, the organic state in practice tends to build mechanisms of control within corporative institutions that are too strong to allow for any meaningful autonomous participation of the working class. That is why in practice organic-statism and corporatism favor the interests of capitalists and the state at the expense of those of the working class.

The mechanisms of control built into the corporative structure through which the Brazilian state controls workers are many and complex. Since I will describe them in detail in the last chapters of this book, I shall not write about them here. At this stage, it is sufficient to note that such mechanisms operate in two distinct ways, only one of which is clearly recognized. It is well known that state-controlled corporative labor systems put a damper on the collective action of workers, especially autonomous action. Such systems therefore greatly curtail the power of workers to make demands—they effectively suppress threatening issues and demands. In other words, corporative institutions *mobilize bias* in favor of the upper classes and against the interest of the lower orders of society.[12]

Less well known is the effect corporative organizations have on the political consciousness of workers. As I shall show in later chapters, the control mechanisms built into those institutions are also mechanisms of socialization. They have the effect of maintaining authoritarian-corporative beliefs among workers. In this sense, they are conducive to the indoctrination of workers with the ideology developed by Brazilian elites that guided the building of the corporative state, the Estado Novo—an ideology Lamounier has called a state ideology.[13]

In this chapter, I shall not show how corporative institutions maintain a state ideology. Nor shall I show how this state ideology acts against the interests of workers. This will be done in the next three chapters. Here I shall only show the congruence between the state ideology of the Estado Novo and the political beliefs of workers in the early seventies. I shall then offer some evidence indicating that Brazilian workers have continuously held authoritarian-corporative beliefs since the thirties. How Brazilian elites indoctrinated workers, and how these beliefs have been maintained since the Estado Novo, are questions that will be dealt with in the three last chapters of this book.

THE AUTHORITARIAN IDEOLOGY OF THE ESTADO NOVO: THE STATE IDEOLOGY

Whatever their differences, the ideologues of the Estado Novo had the same basic objectives.[14] Like many thinkers and politicians of their time, they wanted an alternative to what they thought of as the chaotic politics of liberal democracy, on the one hand, and the stifling rigidity of communist regimes, on the other. Although they were influenced by the authoritarian experiences of Italy and Germany, they preferred to establish in Brazil a form of authoritarian state very different from fascism. The authoritarian corporatism of the Estado Novo was their ideal alternative to liberalism, communism, and fascism.

Like the other authoritarianisms of the time, the Brazilian variant was chiefly a reaction to liberalism. As usual, the authoritarian ideologues criticized the idea that individuals freely pursuing their own interests would generate the most good for society. They did not believe in Adam Smith's invisible hand, that is, in the self-regulating capacity of market society. They argued that the development of capitalism ultimately leads to a high degree of government intervention in the economy. As this occurs, the separation between the economic and the political sphere essential to the proper functioning of liberal societies collapses, and economic competition turns into political conflict. The state becomes a class weapon, and the class struggle is intensified. According to these authoritarian thinkers, the final outcome was thus likely to be the emergence of a communist or fascist state.

Writing in 1938, Azevedo Amaral, one of the major authoritarian thinkers of the thirties, went so far as to claim that industrial societies had to become authoritarian in order to overcome the massive organized conflicts between big corporations and well-organized trade unions that their evolution entailed.[15] He claimed that liberal-democratic politics, or the political market, if you will, cannot resolve such conflicts, since they would merely reflect the social conflict between the narrow private interests of society. Only an authoritarian state free from popular pressure can overcome conflicts of such magnitude, restore harmony, and promote the common good.

Similarly, Francisco Campos, the author of the constitution of the Estado Novo, suggested that the dynamics of liberal systems would intensify the class struggle and could lead to communism.[16] According to him, Marx was correct in predicting that the political and economic liberalism of the capitalist world was suffering a process of decomposition. But, unlike Marx, he thought that this process would not necessarily lead to communism. The corporative state could prevent it:

> Corporatism kills communism as liberalism engenders communism. Corporatism interrupts the process of decomposition of the capitalist world foreseen by Marx as resulting from liberal anarchy. The great political revolutions of the 20th century belied Marx's prophecy and demoralized marxist dialectics. The will of men and their decisions can, therefore, put an end to the supposedly necessary evolution from capitalism to communism. Corporatism, the enemy of communism and, consequently, of liberalism, is the barrier that today's world erected against the moscovite inundation.[17]

According to thinkers like Campos, what was needed was a strong interventionist state that could, at the same time, rise above class interests. Such a state could rise above those interests, however, only if liberal freedoms, parties, and electoral competition were abolished. Otherwise, the interventionist state would be captured by particular interests, and anarchy and communism would follow. Thus, to save the basic aspects of economic liberalism from communism, political liberalism had to be replaced by corporatism, for, the corporative state was a strong interventionist state, which could rise above class interests without destroying the economic institutions of capitalism.

Presumably, then, the corporative state establishes the needed primacy of the collective interest over particular interests, which the liberal state cannot. This is the role the authoritarian ideologues assigned to the Estado Novo. This new corporative state was given the role of transforming Brazilian society into a harmonious, organic whole. But it was to be organic in a way different from communist and fascist systems. These totalitarian states, as Azevedo Amaral called them, were different from corporative ones in that they did not abide by the "principle of subsidiarity."[18] The corporative state is limited in furthering the common good by the idea that all the component parts of society—the individual, the family, and private associations—have their function in the organic whole.[19] The state should therefore refrain from fully penetrating and transforming those subsidiary parts, interfering only when they disrupt the functioning of the organic whole. The authoritarian ideologues of the Estado Novo thus rejected the totalitarian mobilization of communism and fascism. The corporative state was to guide society, not to destroy it.

To be sure, not all Brazilian authoritarians of the thirties were of one mind with Azevedo Amaral and Francisco Campos. As Wanderley G. dos Santos pointed out, the latter were *doctrinary* authoritarians: they thought that authoritarian government was inevitable and would become a permanent feature of modern societies.[20] There was, however, another group of thinkers—the *instrumental* authoritarians, such as Oliveira Vianna and those he influenced, like Virgínio Santa Rosa and Martins de Almeida.[21] For them, the authoritarian state was a transitory means to construct a truly liberal society in fundamentally authoritarian countries like Brazil. Rather than reacting to liberalism as an abstract value, the instrumental authoritarians reacted to its concrete effects on Brazilian society. Oliveira Vianna argued that the liberal constitutions of the Old Republic (1899–1930) had paradoxically strengthened the autocratic rule of the rural oligarchies in the states.[22] Although the Constitution of 1891 had granted universal suffrage, the vote could be easily controlled by the machines of the state oligarchs in what was still a largely rural society. And the federalism of the constitution had given immense powers to the state oligarchies at the expense of the central government. To Oliveira Vianna this meant that the rural oligarchies had appropriated the liberal state to protect their private interests at the expense of the public interest. This situation could be corrected only by recentralizing the system and strengthening the federal government. An authoritarian corporative state such as the Estado Novo was necessary to curb the power of the rural oligarchies in order to construct a genuinely liberal society in the future.

Whatever their differences, however, the authoritarian thinkers of the thirties shared the same views on the need for a corporative state in Brazil. Lamounier constructed a model to represent these views, the ensemble of which he calls the *state ideology*.[23] Lamounier uses this label to stress that Brazilian authoritarian thinkers clearly favored the principle of the state over that of the market as the guiding principle for the organization of political life. They praised the virtues of rational control and deliberate intervention through the coercive hierarchy of a bureaucratic apparatus and denied "any rationality to coordinating mechanisms based on competitive processes or automatic compensatory adjustments."[24] In other words, competition and the self-regulating mechanisms of society should not be trusted. Rather, the guardianship of society should be entrusted to a benevolent state. This benevolent leviathan should be to a society what a father is to his child: it should enhance society's better qualities while gently correcting its bad ones. Such a gentle but firm state should enhance the natural cooperation of an equally benevolent society by shaping it into a harmonious organic whole. It should mold society into an organic-corporative order in which the organs of society, the several social groups, are assigned functions that complement each other, forming a harmonious whole.

Needless to say, these authoritarian thinkers did not think

that political conflict is either inevitable or desirable. As Lamounier put it, they saw conflict as an irrational "manifestation of the childish and malevolent impulses of human nature."[25] The benevolent leviathan would check such impulses, keep conflict to a minimum, and allow the natural cooperative benevolence of society to flourish within the mold of an organic corporative order. Such an order had to be constructed deliberately by means of an objective application of technical knowledge to the problems of Brazilian society. Of course, this technocratic objectivism is profoundly inimical to any form of mass political mobilization and to the spontaneous organization of civil society into autonomous associations, which are seen as both irrational and dangerously uncontrollable. Political parties, interest groups, and electoral politics were all seen as producing the divisive factionalism that disturbed the peaceful cooperative nature of society. Social groups and interests had to be organized by the state in a corporative way, that is, along functional lines, so as to maximize their complementarity and cooperation.

These were the ideas guiding the political elite that created the Estado Novo. This new state was to be their benevolent leviathan. Its authoritarianism, interventionism, and corporatism were to transform Brazil into a great modern nation, respected abroad, and in peaceful harmony within its borders. The new corporative state was to promote peace between social classes. With this intent, the Estado Novo was to arbitrate the relations between labor and capital through a corporative organization of industrial relations. Just as workers were represented by the official labor organization, the *sindicato*, employers were represented by official associations symmetric to those of workers. This symmetry of associations, which was created for each of the main sectors of economic activity, was meant to promote both a functional integration of the economy as well as a collaboration between classes. The leaders of the associations of employers and employees were to represent their constituencies as well as to collaborate with the state in finding solutions that harmonized their interests. As Vargas himself put it, the corporative unions, the *sindicatos,* were not instruments of class struggle but, rather, organizations "for the collaboration of labor and capital with the government."[26] Thus, the political elite of the Estado Novo believed they were erecting a benevolent state that acted in the interests of all classes. This authoritarian elite claimed that by promoting the common good rather than the interests of the upper classes, as the previous regime did, it was also protecting the interests of the downtrodden. And the downtrodden believed this was the case; they saw Vargas as their protector, "the father of the poor." As we shall see, however, they were wrong.

THE POLITICAL VIEWS OF WORKERS

The architects of the Estado Novo hoped that its corporative structure would show workers that this new kind of authoritarian state was in their best interests. Their hopes seem to have materialized. More than three decades after the inauguration of the Estado Novo, two of which passed under a democratic regime, Brazilian urban workers still seemed to subscribe to the organic, corporative, and authoritarian views that form the state ideology.

The urban workers we interviewed in 1972 and 1973 judged regimes and governments by using as their ideal the model laid out by the state ideology of the thirties.[27] They wanted a strong and benevolent government, a benevolent leviathan, to look after them, and were largely indifferent to, or even contemptuous of, electoral politics and politicians. When asked to rank four attributes a government should have, only 13 percent of our respondents ranked "being elected" first. On the other hand, 82 percent ranked either "maintaining order," "being honest," or "being hard-working" as the most important characteristics a government should have.

Workers not only placed little value on electoral politics, but also seemed to believe that such politics get in the way of good government and the achievement of the common good. Like the authoritarian thinkers of the Estado Novo, they seemed to think that political mobilization and competition should be avoided. Government should be free from the pressures and capricious demands of particular interest groups in order to act in the best interest of all. As can be seen from table 1, almost 90 percent of the workers said that, if government paid much attention to the people, the country would relapse into anarchy, and 70 percent thought that workers should not be allowed to strike, even if they had good reason to do so.

Apparently Brazilian workers believed they should not aggressively push their own interests through actions such as strikes, because that would be detrimental to the common good. Rather than having an adversarial relation with the government and their employers, they preferred to be cooperative and let the public interest override their own narrower interests. Almost three decades after the end of the Estado Novo, they behaved as the main architects of the corporative state hoped they would.

The conformity of workers to corporative ideals should not be exaggerated, however. After all, 26 percent of them thought that strikes should be allowed. We also know that Brazilian workers did participate in strikes before and after the military regime. But, although participating in strikes is somewhat against corporative ideals, it does not necessarily entail a rejection of corporative institutions. It can be, rather, a modification

TABLE 1.
Worker Response to Statements on Government, the People, and Strikes
(percent)

Statement	*Agree*	*Neutral*	*Disagree*
If government paid much attention to what the people want, the country would end up in a mess. (N = 535)	89	2	9
Even though they may have good reason, workers should still not be allowed to strike. (N = 501)	70	4	26

SOURCE: Cohen et al., *Representation and Development in Brazil, 1972–1973*.

introduced to provide a corrective for the imperfections of corporative systems. Rather than using the strike to destroy corporative institutions and create autonomous labor organizations, workers may use it to enforce compliance of negligent state officials to the corporative norms of behavior. This seems to be what was meant by most of the minority of Brazilian workers who favored strikes. As is shown below, almost all workers favored the corporative system. Also, Kenneth Erickson's extensive studies of Brazilian strikes showed that workers did strike for economic rather than political reasons. Rather than a greater autonomy from the state, workers wanted the state to perform its protective function.[28]

In exchange for their collaboration, the workers expected the government to look after their interests. Following the authoritarian-corporative scheme, they thought the state should be an all-powerful benevolent leviathan, which made sure their interests were furthered as much as they could be without hampering the collective interest. That workers wanted the state to be their guardian is shown beyond doubt by the figures of table 2. Workers definitely wanted their unions, the corporative *sindicatos*, to be controlled by the government. At the time they were interviewed, the military had imposed even

TABLE 2.
Worker Response to Statements on Government Control of *Sindicatos*
(percent)

Government Should Control Sindicados	*Respondents Who Believed Government Does Control the the* Sindicatos *(N = 288)*	*Respondents Who Believed Government Does Not Control the the* Sindicatos *(N = 76)*
More	69	76
Same	25	19
Less	6	5

SOURCE: Cohen et al., *Representation and Development in Brazil, 1972–1973.*
NOTE: A total of 90 percent of the respondents wanted government to control the *sindicatos*. This total was obtained by adding the number of workers who wanted more control (of both categories) to the number of workers who said government controls *sindicatos* and wanted the same control.

greater government control over the unions, yet almost 90 percent of these workers thought that the government should control unions either to the same extent they were being controlled or even more.

When asked why they wanted government to control the unions, workers confirmed the results of table 1. One of the most frequent reasons given for government control was that it is necessary to prevent political agitation and strikes, which are seen as riotous and anarchic behavior rather than as rational means of exerting pressure. Another frequent answer was that government has to insure that unions are efficiently managed and kept free from corruption. Finally, workers also argued that government control and support of the unions helps bring about better working conditions, more employment, and higher wages.

In a detailed study of both leaders and rank-and-file members of the Brazilian *sindicatos,* Amaury de Souza found similar results.[29] In his analysis, de Souza captured the dramatic nature of the dilemma faced by labor leaders who wanted a greater autonomy for the unions. He showed that such leaders are extremely isolated and are not understood by the majority of workers, who believe in the benevolent character of the state. These leaders, in turn, systematically misperceived the views of workers. Because they were never exposed to a different organization of state-union relations, Brazilian workers seemed unable to perceive the disadvantages of the corporatist unions or the advantages of noncorporatist ones; they seemed unaware of alternatives. This unawareness does not mean that their understanding of the actual function of the unions was completely inaccurate. They took them for what they largely are: extensions of the federal bureaucracies providing welfare services for workers. And this was just what workers wanted them to be. What they did not perceive was that the corporative unions, as we shall see in the next chapter, are also used to control their wages and to preempt the formation of a more powerful labor movement.

The authoritarian-corporative views of workers on the role

of the state are perhaps best seen in workers' answers evaluating the military governments and the democratic government of João Goulart, which preceded the 1964 coup.[30] Goulart's government is often thought of as having acted in the best interest of workers because the president was associated with the left, because he pushed a program of radical and egalitarian reforms, and because he condoned and even encouraged a far more autonomous labor movement. On the other hand, since the military governments not only tightened the corporative controls over the unions and repressed rebellious labor leaders, but also widened the disparity of wealth and decreased real wages in the years after the coup, it is only natural to expect that urban workers would be strongly against them. Consequently, it is often thought that urban workers favored Goulart's government and were strongly opposed to the military regime that followed his deposition. Yet, exactly the opposite occurred. Workers were overwhelmingly in favor of the military governments and against Goulart's government.

The questionnaires are replete with disparaging comments on the lawlessness, anarchic disorder, and demagoguery of Goulart's rule. Instead of seeing the turbulent attempt by a minority of the working class to create a more autonomous labor movement in a favorable light, the majority of workers saw it as destructive agitation that could only serve the interests of demagogues and rabble-rousing communists. While only 3 percent of our respondents said that Goulart and his predecessor, Jânio Quadros, were the best presidents Brazil had since 1930, about 40 percent said that the military presidents were the best, and 42 percent said that Vargas was the best. On the other hand, while about 40 percent said Goulart and his predecessor had been the worst presidents, only 15 percent said the military had been the worst, and a mere 2 percent said Vargas was the worst. Workers thought highly of the military government of the time, the Medici government. When asked whether they were satisfied with it, 44 percent said they were entirely satisfied, 36 percent said they were more or less satisfied, 7 percent were indifferent, and only 5 percent said they were dissatisfied.

Given the views of workers on the role of the state, their preference for the military governments is not as suprising as it seems. Although Goulart pressed for major redistributive reforms and furthered the power of working-class organizations, his government was marked by intense mobilization and conflict as well as by a severe economic crisis. At the time of Goulart's accession to power in 1961, the economy was growing at a rate of 10 percent; shortly before he was ousted, the rate was 1.5 percent. Whereas the inflation rate rose by 50 percent in 1962, it was rising at a rate of over 140 percent in the three-month period before the collapse of Goulart's government.[31] From the many remarks workers made about that period, it is clear that they saw the political turmoil of Goulart's government as the cause of this economic decline. Instead of seeing the general crisis of the time as a temporary price to pay for a restructuring of power relations in their favor, Brazilian workers saw it as a progression toward chaos and hardship. They interpreted what was occurring in terms of the authoritarian-corporative state ideology of the thirties: Goulart's government had succumbed to the play of particular interests. Its partisanship had fostered the mobilization of society and political conflict. Consequently, a strong and benevolent government was needed to restore order, that is, to restore the prevalence of the public interest over the selfish particular interests of society. Brazilian workers thought that the military were doing just that.

By the time of the interviews, the military had reversed the economic situation. Whether or not the military was responsible for such a reversal, the fact is that after the coup Brazil knew one of its periods of higher prosperity, with a simultaneous drastic reduction of inflation.[32] Although the economic situation of the working class continued to deteriorate, workers blamed this on the previous regime and believed that in due time the military would improve their situation as it had already done where the cost of living was concerned. Because their beliefs led them to assume that political mobilization and conflict were detrimental to the common good and could only bring chaos and economic decline, they could not see that under Goulart workers could have become far more powerful and, therefore, could have greatly improved their lot. Nor could they see that the military governments they thought were acting in the interests of workers were in fact reducing inflation at their expense, since they never saw that authoritarianism as well as corporatist unions were actually used to control the wages of the working class. On the contrary, they thought that the military restored to the state its role as the benevolent leviathan. As tables 3 and 4 show, the military government of the time, the Medici government, was the group most trusted by urban workers to defend the interests of the working class.

Clearly, the government and military were the most trusted entities. And, as one would expect from an organic-corporative perspective, politicians were most distrusted. It would seem, then, that workers were as much in favor of the military government because it fulfilled its role as prescribed by the view of the state as a benevolent leviathan as they were against

TABLE 3.
Worker Response to the Question: "Whom Can You Trust to Defend the Interests of People Like You?"
(percent)

	Response per Grade of Trust[a]			
Entity	*0–4*	*5*	*6–10*	*Don't Know*
Government	10	10	71	9
Military	17	12	60	11
Judges	14	11	60	15
Church	20	14	58	8
Boss	24	16	42	18
Unions	21	16	39	24
Politicians (ARENA)[b]	23	15	34	28
Politicians (MDB)[c]	24	16	32	28

SOURCE: Cohen et al., *Representation and Development in Brazil, 1972–1973.*
NOTE: N = 562.
a. Grade: 0 (low trust) to 10 (high trust)
b. Government party: Aliança Renovadora Nacional.
c. Opposition party: Movimento Democrático Brasileiro.

Goulart's government for failing to perform that role. This should not be taken to mean, however, that Brazilian workers were against elections. Most workers favored elections, although, as we saw, they were far from being their priority. As long as electoral politics were not disruptive, workers did not object to them. But whether there are elections or not was largely irrelevant to their evaluation of a government. They preferred the military to the Goulart government not so much because they preferred a nonelectoral system to an electoral one but because they perceived Goulart's government as failing to perform its protective function. The unfortunate part of this story is that by so doing they were perpetuating their own powerlessness.

THE IMPACT OF THE MILITARY ON THE BELIEFS OF WORKERS

It is unlikely that in the eight years between the coup and the time we interviewed our respondents the military had indoctrinated urban workers with the state ideology. I do not think that the Brazilian democratic regime (1945–64) had transformed urban workers into staunch democrats, who were then retransformed into authoritarians by eight years of military dictator-

TABLE 4.
Worker Response to the Question: "Do You Feel You Should Trust or Distrust . . ."
(percent)

Entity	*Always Trust or Trust in Most Cases*	*Trust More or Less*	*Always Distrust or Distrust in Most Cases*	*Don't Know*
Government	70	16	10	4
Military	62	18	14	6
Priests	46	21	30	3
Boss	44	22	26	8
Politicians	20	23	50	7

SOURCE: Cohen et al., *Representation and Development in Brazil, 1972–1973.*
NOTE: N = 562.

ship. If the corporative structure of the Estado Novo had been destroyed by the democratic regime, such a scenario would have been far more likely. But the Brazilian "experiment in democracy" was very peculiar.

As Francisco Weffort has noted, the democratic system that followed Vargas's dictatorship differed radically from the model of democracy known in Western Europe and the United States. In the Brazilian democracy, "all important organizations that mediate between the state and individuals were, in reality, extensions of the state rather than genuinely autonomous organizations."[33] In fact, not only did the corporative organization of labor survive intact the democratic period, the parties that emerged after the end of the Estado Novo also functioned as a cog of the huge machinery of patronage run by the state apparatus. Nathaniel Leff and Maria do Carmo Campello de Souza have shown that the centralization of power effected by Vargas conditioned the parties to function as patronage machines of the federal executive rather than as genuine representative institutions.[34] Throughout the democratic period, the federal executive continued to concentrate power with regard to the major policy decisions and maintained itself well insulated from social pressures. Rather than disrupting the corporative institutions of the Estado Novo, the new democratic institutions were adjusted to what had been, and was to remain, a state-dominated society.

This authoritarian democracy probably encouraged the kinds of beliefs and expectations that were developed under the authoritarian-corporatist context of Vargas's Estado Novo. Urban workers must have thought that elections and parties mostly benefited greedy politicians, who used them to further their own personal ambitions. That this was the case with our respondents is clearly indicated by how little they thought of elections and politicians. But there is also some evidence that urban workers felt this way even before the military regime.

In his study of workers in the automobile industry in São Paulo, Leôncio Martins Rodrigues showed that in 1963 unskilled workers clearly preferred dictatorship to democracy.[35] It was only the minority of highly skilled workers that preferred a democratic form of government. Just like our respondents, most workers opted for authoritarian forms of government because, as Rodrigues put it, "dictatorship is seen as being the best way of obtaining an honest and decent government, which is capable of defending workers against the bad politicians and exploiting merchants."[36] Not surprisingly, many workers wanted a dictatorship like that of Vargas.

There are also other reasons to believe that workers could not have been so thoroughly indoctrinated by the military. A consistent finding of research on attitude change is that those who show little involvement with politics are among those least susceptible to influence, because they rarely pay attention to political communications.[37] Since 80 percent of our respondents said they took no interest in politics and 84 percent said politics was too complicated for them to follow, it can be safely concluded that they probably paid little attention to the political communications of the military. In other words, their attitudes were probably unaffected by the military governments. Had their attitudes been changed by the military, however, one would expect older workers to be more democratic than the younger. Yet there is hardly any relation between indicators of authoritarian corporatism and age of respondent.[38]

All of these results suggest that the attitudes of Brazilian urban workers have been rather stable since the Estado Novo. It seems that the democratic period did not change the predilection of urban workers for the benevolent leviathan, which is central to the state ideology. In one sense, their negative views of political parties, the electoral system, and the politicians were accurate, for these never gave much power to the workers. Yet, in another sense, their perception reinforced their dependence on the state, for they failed to perceive that the ineffectiveness of democratic procedures in the Brazilian context was in part due to the overwhelming power of the state. Since their concrete experience with elections stressed the irrelevance of elections to their lives, most workers could not see them as what they could be, that is, as effective instruments of power. It is the same with corporative unions. Workers took them for what they are, but they did not see that they could become genuine autonomous working-class organizations should the state lose its grip over them. At the level of their consciousness, a strange but understandable inversion had taken place: because workers did not see the source of their dependence in the action of the state, they saw it as their rescuer and benefactor instead of seeing it as their oppressor.

Chapter 4

THE INTERESTS OF WORKERS

I HAVE NOW provided some evidence showing that, at least up to the early seventies, Brazilian workers preferred authoritarian-corporative forms of government. They believed that strong authoritarian governments are more benevolent than democratic ones where workers and the poor are concerned. Whereas they associated authoritarian-corporative institutions with order, honesty, efficiency, and prosperity, they clearly distrusted democratic politics, which they saw as breeding disorder, corrupt politicians, mismanagement, and economic disaster rather than as affording them a better chance to improve their lot. Democratic politics only gave demagogues a chance to fool and exploit workers. According to Brazilian workers, only an authoritarian, orderly, and efficient government actively promoting the public good would benefit them.

Whether this preference for an authoritarian-corporative state is justified is far from clear, however. In this chapter I shall argue that it is not—that the workers were mistaken. The government of their preference acts against their interests. In order to show this, I must first say what I mean by *interests* and discuss how one can know whether some belief or action is in the interest of individuals.

THE CONCEPT OF INTEREST

I am here concerned only with one of the senses of the term *interest.* That sense is the one we give to the term when we say that something is in someone's interest. To say this is to say that something is to someone's advantage, good, or profit. Of course, everyone agrees that this is one of the meanings of the word interest. The disagreement is not about the meaning of the word. It is, rather, about the possibility of making a mistake concerning one's interest.

On the one hand, there are those to whom it makes no sense to say that someone made a choice that was *not* in his interest. According to this view of interest, each of us is the only and best judge of his own interest.[1] In this sense no one can mistake his interest; no one can choose badly in relation to his interest. If a person chooses to support a given policy, or prefers a certain social arrangement to another, it must be because these are in his best interest. From this perspective, there is no single set of criteria allowing us to judge what is for someone else's good. I have mine and you have yours. I cannot therefore tell you that your preference for socialism shows that you have mistaken your interest. If you choose socialism, it must be because it is in your interest.

From this perspective, the authoritarian-corporative state is in Brazilian workers' interest, since they prefer it to other state forms. According to this perspective, there are no objective criteria according to which one can make judgments about the interest of others. No one can be better qualified to pronounce on what is in a person's interest than that person himself. This is why this perspective is referred to as a *subjectivist* view of interest, a view that rejects the argument that there are objective or public criteria for judging the "rightness" of a person's preference. This view is attributed to liberal theory, or some formulations of it, and to its heirs, the so-called pluralists.

In one sense, however, it is not entirely true that pluralists subscribe to this extreme form of subjectivism. Although pluralists are clearly subjectivists, they do admit of one possibility of mistaking one's interests.[2] They agree with Brian Barry that people can mistake their interests only in the sense that they can be mistaken about how some policy, behavior, or belief affects their opportunity to get what they want.[3] In this sense, I can say to a man who wants to be wealthy that he has mistaken his interest if he clearly makes a factual error concerning the investment of his money. But I cannot pronounce about his interest in being wealthy. That remains entirely up to him; it still is a subjective judgment. Thus the judgment about the means is objective, that about the ends continues to be subjective. According to this variation on a subjectivist view, we can say that someone has mistaken his interest only where the instrumental value of things is concerned, never when it comes to his noninstrumental values. Whereas we could say that Brazilian workers make a mistake in supporting an authoritarian regime because such a regime affects their wages negatively, we could not say that they are mistaking their interest because authoritarianism is a bad thing in itself, irrespective of whatever instrumental value it may have. From this adjusted subjectivist point of view, then, we can say that someone has mistaken his interest but we can only do so if we know his wants beforehand. This is still a subjectivist view, however, in that its proponents still reject the argument that ultimate wants and values can be judged objectively.

At the other extreme are those who argue that people can be mistaken about what is in their interest even when the noninstrumental value of things is involved. Isaac Balbus, William Connolly, Steven Lukes, and Grenville Wall, to mention some of the most prominent recent defenders of this view, all have argued that there are objective criteria by which we can judge the rightness of someone's choice, even when it comes to the value of things in themselves, irrespective of their instrumental value.[4] Those who hold this *objectivist* view of interest argue that an observer can decide what is in someone's interest regardless of what this person thinks is in his interest. According to them, people not only make factual mistakes from means to ends but also make mistaken *value* judgments about their own interests. This means that others are often better qualified to judge what is in my or your interest. Objectivists are therefore willing to pronounce on whether health, wealth, equality, or freedom, as goods in themselves, are in someone's interest. As Wall has noted, such a perspective must claim that "moral judgments are objective and capable of rational justification."[5] In order to say that judgments about one's interests are not merely private ones, objectivists must claim that there are *public* criteria of rightness or correctness by which others can make judgments about the rightness or correctness (that is, moral judgments) about our choices.

Although I believe it is possible to argue that authoritarian-corporative institutions are not in the interest of Brazilian workers from an objectivist perspective, I shall not do so here. Presumably one could construct an argument against corporative institutions by arguing that their manipulative character is morally unacceptable. As we shall see, corporative institutions keep workers politically ignorant, dependent and servile, all of which could be said to be against the interests of Brazilian workers. One would therefore conclude that Brazilian workers mistake their interests in supporting corporative institutions.

Rather than arguing in this way, I shall take the less controversial tack of making only an instrumental judgment of authoritarian-corporative institutions. Without rejecting the objectivist view, I will here follow the strategy suggested by Brian Barry's subjectivism. As we saw, Barry argued that we must first know the wants of people before we can say that they have mistaken their instrumental interests. In our case, this would mean knowing what Brazilian workers want before we can say whether their support for corporative institutions furthers their interest or not. This is easy to do where their material wants are concerned. As we saw, Brazilian workers want to improve their lot, and they see the corporative state as best achieving this end. Thus, if we show that they are mistaken—that is, that corporative arrangements prevent workers from improving their material condition—we shall have some reason to say that such arrangements are not in their interest and that workers are therefore mistaken about their true interests.

The second argument I want to advance is more problematic. It requires saying that Brazilian workers do not want to be manipulated. It is possible to show that corporative arrangements are of a manipulative nature because they hide from workers the negative effect they have on them.[6] Corporative institutions keep workers in the dark, they keep them politically unaware. Assuming that workers do not want to be manipulated, one could then say that they are mistaken about their interests when they support the corporative state. The trouble, however, is that I do not know whether workers care about being manipulated. I suppose that I can therefore be accused of arbitrarily imputing interests to Brazilian workers. I will nevertheless make this argument because I suspect that most human beings find utterly repulsive the kind of political manipulation to which Brazilian workers are subjected. But I can always be proven wrong, since it is possible to gather evidence on how workers feel about political manipulation and under what conditions they would be willing to accept it. Meanwhile, I will assume that they do not want to be manipulated.

In the following pages, I will first examine the evidence concerning the effect of authoritarian-corporative institutions on the material conditions of workers. I will then argue that these institutions are designed in such a way as to allow a manipulation of workers that ultimately serves the interests of Brazilian elites far better than those of Brazilian workers.

AUTHORITARIANISM, CORPORATISM, AND WORKING-CLASS WAGES

As we saw in the previous chapter, Brazilian workers were discontented with Goulart's government, the democratic government that was ousted by the military. From the very beginning of his government, Goulart was strongly opposed by powerful sectors of the Brazilian ruling elites.[7] To stay in power and push through his program of reforms, he had to increasingly rely on militant and radical labor leaders and their following among workers in the large cities. This allowed the more militant leaders to gain a considerable measure of power within the corporative labor system as well as to form their own independent parallel organizations outside the official structure.[8] Through these organizations, radical labor leaders were better able to coordinate the demonstrations and strikes in the larger urban centers that further enhanced the incipient autonomy of the labor movement.[9] On the other hand, however, the growing power of the left and the mobilization of the still relatively small number of disgruntled workers frightened moderates and provoked a bitter reaction from the right. Consequently, the last months of Goulart's government were marked by high degrees of polarization and mobilization.[10] Many city dwellers took to the streets both to defend and to attack Goulart; protest demonstrations and strikes were common.

Such turbulence not only frightened the middle and upper classes but also the great majority of workers. As our interviews show, rather than seeing the mobilization of militant workers as leading to an increasing power of the working class that would ultimately improve their lot, most workers saw it as generating purposeless anarchy and violence. The only people who could gain from all of that agitation, they thought, were its instigators, the corrupt demagogues and the dangerous communist agitators, all of whom had benefited from Goulart's weakness and ineptitude. As we have already seen, most workers were therefore relieved when the military ousted Goulart. They expected the military to regain control and to rid Brazil of political inefficiency and corruption and of communist agitation.

Their views were reinforced by the rapid deterioration of the economy under Goulart's administration.[11] Although the economic decline of those years had multiple causes and had only a minor effect on working-class wages, workers saw it exclusively as resulting from the ineptitude, corruption, and anarchy of Goulart's government. They saw it as confirming the authoritarian-corporative belief that the haggling of democratic politics ultimately leads to chaos and economic decline. That is why they supported the military; they saw it as a means to restore order to the Brazilian polity. By ridding Brazil of demagogues, corrupt politicians, inefficient administrators, and communist agitators, it would reestablish order, and prosperity would follow. It is no wonder that these workers were so supportive of the military in 1972. At that time, the economy was growing at what was thought of as a miraculous rate, and inflation was at a record low.[12] Although the recovery was achieved at the expense of workers' wages and was not solely due to the return to authoritarian corporatism, it appeared once again to confirm the beliefs of workers.

In one respect, the civilian and military coup makers had the same views and concerns of the workers. They blamed inflation and economic decline largely on the profligate spending of demagogic politicians, on the ineptitude of old-fashioned populist politicians such as Goulart, on the corruption they thought characterized populist government, and on the chaos produced by what they thought were dangerous communist agitators.[13] So they saw their mission as fighting corruption and communism by ridding Brazil of demagogues and agitators and fighting ineptitude by substituting the technocrat for the populist politician. In order to perform these tasks, the "revolutionaries" of 1964 used a new weapon, which increased the power of the Brazilian executive in an unprecedented way. They issued a series of institutional acts that granted the executive the power to issue practically any rule it decreed in the national interest, to deprive recalcitrant citizens of their political rights, and to cancel the mandates of undesirable elective officers.[14] Between 1964 and 1974, about 5,000 persons were purged (500 of whom were elective officers, who lost their mandates and their political rights for ten years) and thousands were incarcerated and tortured.[15]

Together with the Constitution of 1967 and the amendments of 1969, the institutional acts sharply reduced the power of the Congress and the judiciary and dismantled the party system, thus preventing the possibility of even the mildest opposition to military rule. The First Institutional Act arbitarily declared that, rather than the Congress bestowing legitimacy, the Congress received its legitimacy from the military "as a result of the exercise of the Constituent Power inherent in all revolutions."[16] As such, the act allowed the military to cancel legally the mandate of one-fifth of the federal legislators elected in 1962 and to withdraw the political rights of as many as 2,489 persons.[17]

To prevent genuine opposition to the regime, the Second Institutional Act (1965) abolished all existing political parties and created an official government party, the ARENA, as well as an official opposition party, the MDB. In addition, it established indirect elections of the president, vice-president, state governors, and mayors of state capital cities. The selection of the first three was transferred from the electorate to the corresponding legislative body, which was controlled by the military, and mayors were nominated by state governors.[18]

Subsequent emergency acts as well as the Constitution of 1967 and its 1969 amendments virtually eliminated any impact on decision making the Congress may have had.[19] Bills submitted to the Congress were to be acted upon in ninety days, and in forty if they were labeled urgent. Otherwise, they automatically became law. Thus, to pass a bill all the majoritarian government party had to do was to induce a lack of quorum. In case this was insufficient, the executive could also suspend the Congress. Given these rules and the systematic purges, it is not surprising that the power of the Congress steadily declined. But that is not all.

The military also purged the Supreme Court of "subversive" judges and exercised control over the media.[20] The press law of 1967 permitted the military to imprison media personnel, to delete copy they did not like, and to seize entire issues of newspapers they did not wish to see in circulation. In short, the ruling military thoroughly destroyed the democratic system that had been in operation since 1946. Because of this, some scholars have seen the coup of 1964 as a restoration movement, that is, as a movement back to the Estado Novo.[21] This it was, but it was even worse. For the military had better means of control than Vargas and used them not only to create a ruthless authoritarian system but also to tighten its grip over the corporative labor structure created by Vargas.

The corporative system had never been abolished; it survived almost intact into the two decades of democracy in Brazil. During Goulart's government, however, it was seriously eroded, to the distress, as we saw, not only of the traditional ruling elites and the military but also of the majority of workers. Goulart had chosen not to apply the legal sanctions prescribed by the corporative labor legislation against more militant labor leaders. He allowed them to form parallel organizations and to use strikes in ways that could clearly be considered illegal.

As soon as it seized power, the military therefore resorted to a strict application of the corporative laws to eliminate the incipient radical labor movement. Foremost among the available legal weapons was the right of government to intervene in labor oganizations whose leaders allegedly violated the law.[22] Since the language of the law is vague, it was very easy for the Ministry of Labor to intervene against recalcitrant unions. In this way, the military government was able to replace a sizable militant labor leadership with passive progovernment appointees in a relatively short period of time. The first military government seized union headquarters and funds and replaced elected officials by government appointees in no less than 67 percent of the confederations, 42 percent of the federations, and 19 percent of the *sindicatos.*[23] As for prospective candidates, they were now carefully scrutinized by the political police. Those having affiliations of any kind with political organizations banned by the new regime were forbidden to run for office, the same being true, of course, of those who had lost their political rights.

In addition to the purges in the unions, the government changed the social security system to prevent radical labor leaders and the left from using it to create a more autonomous labor movement.[24] As Erickson has shown, during Goulart's government the immense resources of the social security system had increasingly come under the control of the left.[25] In exchange for their support, Goulart gave major figures of the movement for social reform top positions within the federal government. The radical leaders, in turn, used their power to place radical labor leaders in the social security institutes. These were run by tripartite councils, with equal votes for labor, management, and the government. Since these boards commanded valuable resources in the form of jobs and scarce services, the newly empowered radical labor leaders could use them to expand their power over workers. In other words, the social security system provided the left with several sources of patronage that had traditionally been used by labor leaders for their own personal aggrandizement. The left was now putting such patronage to a different use—the creation of an autonomous labor movement and the achievement of sweeping reforms. As soon as the military seized power, they combined all the institutes into the National Social Welfare Institute, run by a government-appointed director; the policy-making body for this system, the National Social Welfare Department, was still run by a tripartite body, although now the government had four directors on the board, while business and labor had only two each.

Aside from the purges and the restructuring of the social security system, in 1964 the military government enforced strike laws in order to prevent any resistance to their austere stabilization programs.[26] The labor law had always given government the power to control strikes. According to the law, workers could not strike without previous authorization from the regional labor court. Penalties for noncompliance were quite severe. Since the government had much control over the appointed labor judges, it was relatively easy for the government to regulate strike activity. But because Goulart needed the support of the militant labor leaders, his government chose not to enforce the strike law. As a consequence, strikes were relatively frequent under his government, increasing from 180 in 1961 to 302 in 1963.[27] The military reversed this pattern by strictly enforcing the law. Under the military, labor courts authorized strikes only to force employers to pay back wages they refused to pay or to pay legal increases they chose to ignore. The role of strikes in pressuring management in negotiating new contracts was completely eliminated. Therefore, the number of strikes dropped to twenty-five in 1965, fifteen in 1966, twelve in 1970, and zero in 1971.[28]

In one sense, then, the military acted in ways workers wished for and expected: it restored order and controlled the unions. Yet, in another sense, it was fooling the workers. Whereas Brazilian workers assumed the military implemented policies that favored them, the policies adopted after 1964 were obviously against the interests of workers. Whereas most workers thought that the restoration of an authoritarian-corporative order was necessary to allow the military to adopt policies that would benefit them, the military restored that order so as to eliminate any source of resistance from the more militant sector of the working class to its highly inegalitarian stabilization program. To put it briefly, most workers were deceived by the military because their authoritarian-corporative views led them to assume that the military and the political order it was imposing could only be favorable to workers as well as to all other Brazilian citizens.

But the policies adopted by the military were far less favorable to the workers than to those higher up in the social hierarchy. The military managed to reduce inflation and resume growth largely at the expense of workers, whose real wages declined drastically.[29] After the coup, the military adopted an automatic wage-setting procedure, which systematically raised wages to below the level of inflation. After implementing several ways of correcting the minimum wage for inflation, all of which led to reductions in real wages, in July 1966 the government issued a decree that transformed the wage-setting process into a purely automatic procedure. Each year, the minimum wage was to be revised according to a rigid formula, which was to be applied and enforced by the labor courts. This procedure did not compensate for the systematic underestimation of inflation, and furthermore, it was not strictly followed by the government.[30] Minimum-wage revisions have been on average almost 4 percent below what they should have been had the formula been applied.[31]

The drastic decline in real wages can be seen in table 5. In the ten years following Goulart's ascension to power in 1961, the real minimum wage dropped to a staggering 60 percent of what it had been at the beginning of the period.[32] Similarly, as shown in table 6, the worker's share of national income declined steadily after the military coup. That the military were clearly acting against the interests of workers is further confirmed by its behavior after the dizzying growth of the economy after 1968. As José Serra has pointed out, the military government did not

TABLE 5.
Index of Annual Average Real Monthly Minimum Wage, Guanabara, 1952–1975

Year	*Index*[a]
1952	95
1953	83
1954	115
1955	113
1956	105
1957	134
1958	101
1959	115
1960	100
1961	115
1962	100
1963	92
1964	90
1965	82
1966	76
1967	75
1968	73
1969	71
1970	69
1971	69
1972	71
1973	75
1974	70
1975	75

SOURCE: Erickson, *Brazilian Corporative State and Working-Class Politics*, p. 165.
a. 1960 = 100.

have to maintain the official policy of severe wage restraint.[33] Between 1968 and 1974, inflation was stabilized at a remarkably low level, and the annual average growth rate of the economy was above the high level of 10 percent, reaching 14 percent in 1973. Even during this period, however, the military did nothing to improve the position of wage earners.

There is no doubt, then, that the authoritarian-corporative restoration conducted by the military was against the interests of workers. The military used authoritarian and corporative institutions to freeze the wages of workers, preventing any resistance from the minority of aware and militant workers to the official policy of severe wage restraint. The majority of workers could not see what the military was doing largely because of their political views, which were reinforced by the miraculous recovery of the economy. Instead of seeing the more militant and radical minority of workers as protecting their interests, most workers saw them as the source of their problems. Instead of seeing the movement for reforms and the struggle for autonomous labor organizations that occurred under Goulart as beneficial, most workers saw them as hampering their interests. Instead of seeing the military as acting against workers' material interests, most workers saw it as furthering their interests. In spite of the fact that their wages were reduced during the first years of the military regime, they still believed that the military was going to improve their situa-

TABLE 6.
Concentration of Income in Brazil, 1960 –1976

Economically Active Population, by Wealth		*Share of Annual Income (percent)*		
		1960	*1970*	*1976*
Richest	5 percent	28	35	39
	15 percent	26	27	28
	30 percent	28	23	21
Poorest	50 percent	18	15	12

SOURCE: Alves, *Estado e Oposição no Brasil (1964–1984)*, p. 149.

tion and blamed Goulart for all their troubles. When economic recovery came, Brazilian workers thought that their beliefs were confirmed. They were optimistic in spite of their difficulties because they thought that the authoritarian-corporative regime was finally coming to their rescue—when, in fact, it had come to prevent them from gaining power and improving their material situation.

A TRADE-OFF BETWEEN ORDER AND WAGES?

A natural objection to my argument is that it does not take into account other wants of workers that may be in conflict with their desire for better material conditions. Since political order is so important to Brazilian workers, it can be argued that in preferring the military regime they were making a perfectly informed, rational, and realistic choice: workers may have been willing to accept lower wages in exchange for a more orderly political environment.

But no such exchange was in the minds of workers when they expressed support for the military. As we saw, they preferred authoritarian regimes precisely because they believed that more order generates greater prosperity and higher wages. As Brazilian workers saw it, the democratic regime had brought disorder, economic decline, and lower wages. On the other hand, the military regime was, in their eyes, both restoring order *and* gradually improving their material situation.

If no trade-off between order and wages was in the minds of workers, it certainly was present in the reality of the Brazilian situation. For the greatest part of the democratic period, the economic situation of workers was much better precisely because a small minority of militant workers was able to press for higher wages. Of course, this meant that wage increases were obtained at the cost of some disorder. Conversely, during the military regime the economic conditions of workers worsened considerably because the military clamped down on the activities of militants. In reality, order came at the expense of lower wages.

Brazilian workers did not see it that way, however. The biases of the state ideology led them to see the progressive deterioration of their situation as a delayed effect of the disorder they associated with democratic government, rather than as a result of current military policy. In the same way, the state ideology led workers to believe that the success of the military in promoting economic growth and curbing inflation was benefiting them when, in fact, this was achieved at the expense of working-class wages.

It is true that for a brief moment—under Goulart—democracy did generate much political turmoil, which ultimately had a negative effect on the economy. On the other hand, the labor movement gained much power under Goulart. Nevertheless, one could always say that workers had good reason to dislike Goulart's government. To dislike Goulart, however, is not necessarily to dislike democracy. It was their beliefs—the state ideology—that led workers to see Goulart's government as a typical instance of democratic politics. In fact, it was not so: during the years before Goulart, democracy had brought much improvement to workers without generating an inordinate amount of disorder.

Had it not been for the state ideology, Brazilian workers would have realized a trade-off had to be made between order and wages. They probably would have realized that democracy is far more likely than autocracy to generate the mix of political order and material conditions they want. Although most workers might still have said that Goulart's was a bad government, they would not have said that democratic governments are worse than authoritarian ones; and they would not have been in favor of the military regime.

AUTHORITARIAN-CORPORATISM AND MANIPULATION

Why were workers unable to see that the restoration of the authoritarian-corporative order was clearly against their best interest? Why were most of them unable to see that the restoration of the corporative labor system that had begun to function in a more autonomous way deprived them of the only source of resistance against the damaging economic policies of the military?

The answer to these questions will be given in the next two chapters. Here I shall limit myself to saying that corporative beliefs and corporative institutions themselves hide from workers their effects on workers. They do so by inhibiting collective action, especially that of an autonomous kind. This in turn prevents workers from acquiring information and knowledge about their political environment. In this way, Brazilian workers are prevented from learning about the true nature of the corporative state. Authoritarian-corporative institutions thus perpetuate themselves largely by keeping workers ignorant about how these institutions actually work. Therein lies their manipulative character, which I shall try to reveal in the rest of the book.

As I said before, my assumption is that if workers understood the manipulative character of corporative institutions they would be against them. But even if I am wrong, and workers would not mind being manipulated, this would not necessarily invalidate my claim that corporative institutions are manipulative, in that they prevent workers from seeing their negative effects. Neither would it invalidate my claim that such institutions perpetuate corporative beliefs and keep workers ignorant about their political environment.

The claim that corporative institutions are not in the interests of workers because they manipulate them is different from the simpler claim that corporative institutions are manipulative. The first claim entails that workers do not want to be manipulated, while the second clearly does not. In this chapter, I make the first claim, and I assume rather than show that workers do not want to be manipulated. In the next chapters, I shall make the second claim, and I will try to demonstrate that corporative institutions keep workers in the dark, thus making them an easy target of manipulation.

Chapter 5

MECHANISMS OF POWER

THE QUESTION that now emerges is why Brazilian workers adopted the authoritarian views of political elites. The question poses itself because one would expect workers to be strongly opposed to those views. As we saw, the authoritarian-corporative beliefs of the state ideology are against their best interest. We thus would expect workers at least to reject the political ideas of the elites if they cannot rebel against them. Yet Brazilian workers not only do not rebel but also accept the values of those who perpetuate their powerlessness and deprivation. As we shall see, powerful mechanisms are at work to prevent them from seeing that the state ideology is against their interests. Before describing those specific mechanisms, however, it will prove useful to discuss power mechanisms in general.

THE SUPPRESSION OF CONFLICT

The most familiar mechanisms of power are those used in open conflict over the resolution of issues that have reached public decision-making arenas. In these cases, each of the parties in conflict uses a variety of resources—votes, jobs, information, connections, experience, organizational strength, and other resources of the kind—to threaten, manipulate, or coopt the others in order to maximize its own self-defined interests. But power resources and mechanisms are not used only to prevail in the resolution of issues that have reached decision-making arenas. They can also be used to suppress issues and conflicts that are threatening to decision makers and the powerful groups with whom they are connected.[1] Instead of struggling to have their way in public arenas such as the courts or the Congress, powerful groups may prevent issues from arising altogether. As Peter Bachrach and Morton Baratz have argued, "demands for change in the allocation of benefits and privileges in the community can be suffocated before they are voiced, or kept covert; or killed before they gain access to the relevant decision-making arena."[2]

There are several mechanisms by which issues and conflict can be suppressed. The most extreme is force. To prevent challenging demands from entering the political process, rebels can be harassed, imprisoned, beaten, or killed, as were civil rights workers in the United States, antiapartheid workers in South Africa, and dissidents in the Soviet Union. In less extreme fashion, challenging demands can be thwarted by threatening to punish the potential initiators of change and promising them rewards for their quiescence. Challengers are reminded that if they persist they may lose their jobs, for instance, or find themselves without bank credit, or otherwise be deprived of essential means for survival.

A third mechanism by which challengers may be prevented from bringing threatening demands into the political process is the invocation of existing norms, precedents, rules, or procedures of the political system that can either delegitimize or deflect such demands. As Bachrach and Baratz put it, demands can "be denied legitimacy by being branded socialistic, unpatriotic, immoral, or in violation of an established procedure."[3] They can also be deflected by referring them "to committees or commissions for detailed and prolonged study or by steering them through time-consuming and ritualistic routines that are built into the political system."[4] A fourth and related mechanism involves changing, or adding, to the rules and procedures of the political system. For example, strike laws can be toughened to prevent strikes, requirements for party formation can be increased to prevent challengers from having a legitimate permanent political existence, or the "demand of rent-strikers can be blunted or dulled by insisting that tenant-landlord relations are a purely private matter."[5]

All of these mechanisms can be used to prevent the powerless and the underprivileged from bringing their demands into the political process. Combined, they are powerful enough to inflict continual defeat on the powerless. Over time, continual defeats can give rise to the operation of a fifth mechanism, which may lead the powerless to withdraw into complete apathy. Through the phenomenon of anticipated reactions, continual defeat is bound to destroy even the will to merely voice grievances. At first, the powerless may withdraw in a calculated way so as to avoid the defeat they think will result from the reactions they anticipate the powerful will have. Over time, however, this calculated withdrawal may lead to an unconscious pattern of withdrawal maintained by the sense of powerlessness within the underdog, regardless of what his objective chances of influence may be.[6] The continual operation of mechanisms to suppress threatening issues and demands can thus ultimately lead to the complete resignation and apathy of the powerless.

The mechanisms involved in defeating the powerless in decision-making arenas and in suppressing their threatening demands do not exhaust the range of mechanisms of power available to elites. Elites can go even beyond preventing grievances and demands from being voiced. They can, so to speak, suppress the very feeling of a grievance. They can do so by persuading the socially deprived that the social order is just and that therefore they have no legitimate reason to even feel the need for change. The mechanism of power involved here can be referred to as *political socialization,* or alternatively, as *indoctrination.* Both terms refer to the process by which beliefs and values about the political order are instilled in the members of a political community. But, whereas the term *socialization* stresses the beneficial consequences of the process for the whole community, *indoctrination* points to its beneficial consequences only for the privileged minority.[7] Rather than seeing the process as one by which individuals are integrated into the community, those who see it as indoctrination see it as the process by which the powerful "teach the disadvantaged to accept their disadvantages."[8] Since this is the aspect of the process that interests us here, I shall refer to it as indoctrination. The remainder of this chapter will discuss this specific mechanism.

THE INDOCTRINATION OF THE LOWER CLASSES

There is much evidence suggesting that the socially deprived are taught to accept their disadvantages. This acceptance is a universal phenomenon; it can be observed throughout the world, from the most traditional to the most modern societies, and from the most tyrannical autocracy to the most benign forms of democracy. The downtrodden accept their fate in caste societies, in fascist polities, in communist ones, as well as in the most liberal of the liberal democracies.[9]

In India, for instance, the Untouchables live in abhorrent conditions and perform the most degrading acts one can imagine.[10] They live in abominable filth and occupy the most degrading position in village life. Members of the higher castes regard them with disgust and will not visit their quarters in the village. The Untouchables perform the most disgusting as well as the hardest tasks in Indian society. They clean the latrines, which means climbing down into the places where the excrement is dropped and carting it away on their heads. They clean the streets, and they remove the carcasses of dead animals, remove their skins for leatherwork, and eat the flesh. Untouchables have also formed a large part of the overworked army of agricultural laborers.

The Untouchables are not forced at gunpoint to live in this way. They do so largely because they have internalized the dominant Hindu beliefs about fate and the transmigration of souls as well as those about cleanliness and pollution. Hindu beliefs about fate and transmigration of souls see the conditions of one's present life on earth as the result of preceding lives. The misfortunes of this life are the result of transgressions in the preceding life, the rewards that of good behavior in the previous incarnation. By behaving well, then, Untouchables hope to improve their standing in the next life. Behaving well, of course, includes conformity to the caste system, that is, committing no transgressions against Brahmans.

The Untouchables also accept beliefs about pollution. Belief in pollution reinforces the political and economic distinctions of the caste system. This system is basically a series of status gradations between purity and holiness at one extreme and degradation and pollution at the other. Since pollution is something to be avoided, the function of the concept is to conceal the disagreeable aspects of society from the higher castes, which also helps to enforce the caste system. The Untouchables accept beliefs about pollution and enforce it among themselves. They are themselves divided into subcastes with various grades of uncleanliness. The higher Untouchable castes loathe the pure Untouchables, who are thought to pollute merely by their touch.

The Indian Untouchables are by no means unique. In a society as different from India as is the United States, those at the bottom of the hierarchy also hold beliefs that make them accept their condition. The American Untouchables, the poor and the black, believe that what they get is what they deserve. In spite of the blatant upper-class biases of capitalist democracy, the lower classes accept the beliefs of dominant elites concerning the fairness of the American system.[11] In spite of ample evidence showing that the American democratic system, like other capitalist democracies, is rigged against the subordinate classes, empirical studies show over and over again that the members of such classes are full of praise for the fairness of the political institutions of their country.[12] Members of the lower classes also equate liberty and equality of opportunity to democracy and see private enterprise as inextricably linked to them.

The same is true of their views on the economic system. In

spite of much evidence to the contrary, the underprivileged believe that the capitalist system offers everyone the same opportunity for advancement. In spite of evidence showing that American capitalism gives tremendous advantages to the offspring of the upper classes, the majority of the underprivileged believe that inequalities in wealth, prestige, and power in American society are desirable and based on merit; that there is unlimited opportunity for advancement; and that therefore individuals get what they deserve.[13]

In 1959, Robert Lane reported that the American men he interviewed believed there was equality of opportunity in the United States.[14] More than twenty years later, the beliefs of Americans about inequality were essentially the same. After interviewing more than 2,000 Americans in 1980, James Kluegel and E. R. Smith concluded that most Americans "believe that economic inequality in principle is necessary and desirable," and that "opportunity for economic advancement is present for all who work hard."[15] They also found that most Americans believe that "most Americans get what they deserve relative to their individual efforts and talents."[16] Perhaps the most surprising piece of evidence is that the same is true of the underprivileged. Although blacks were more critical than whites, and lower classes more so than the upper classes, both race and class differences were rather small.[17] The majority of the underprivileged in the United States clearly internalize the values of the upper class. They do so even in the face of a great deal of divulged evidence showing that there is little equality of opportunity in American society. Although it may be that the lower classes in the United States have been more extensively indoctrinated than their counterparts in European capitalist democracies, there is plenty of evidence showing that in Europe, too, upper-class values are widely internalized by the underprivileged.[18]

Needless to say, members of the lower classes are not forced at gunpoint to absorb the dominant beliefs and values of capitalist democracy. Rather, they learn them very early, at home. Ironically, the underprivileged themselves are turned into major agents of indoctrination by passing on to their children the values of the upper classes. One study after another shows that lower-class children are taught by their parents and their teachers the prevailing upper-class values of their societies.[19]

This routinized, almost automatic indoctrination of the lower classes is reinforced through the other major institutions in charge of disseminating social values. Newspapers and broadcasting systems, schools and universities, religious associations and political organizations are all dependent on the resources coming from wealth, power, and prestige.[20] And, as Lindblom and others have noted, ambitious managers of the media, as well as journalists, schoolteachers, textbook writers, and the faculty and administrators of the universities, have a strong incentive to disseminate the beliefs and values of dominant elites.[21] Their professional advancement is enhanced by their own conformity. Government officials, too, have an incentive to join in the dissemination of dominant values. The last thing they want is to see such values turn into hot political issues.[22] They have a strong interest in maintaining order and prosperity and are therefore threatened by demands for fundamental change by the underprivileged.

The lower-class family is the major instrument of indoctrination not only because it routinely disseminates the prevailing values to its offspring but also because it promotes conformity to external authority.[23] Compared to the socialization of middle- and upper-class children, that of children from the lower classes fosters little autonomous, self-directed behavior. Whereas the relatively higher degree of role differentiation, the more democratic forms of parental control, and the more permissive and participatory strategies of socialization characteristic of middle- and upper-class families promote self-directed behavior among children, the role segregation, authoritarian control, and rigid and restrictive strategies of lower-class families promote outer-directed behavior among their children. In other words, lower-class children are trained not to question authority.

Patterns of socialization also affect the development of linguistic and cognitive skills. Basil Bernstein and others have shown that the linguistically deprived environment of lower-class children limits and arrests the development of their innate linguistic and cognitive skills. The categories of the language of the underprivileged narrow their ability to conceptualize and analyze their condition as being largely determined by the structure of the society in which they live. Their language code thus prevents them from articulating their grievances as social problems legitimately deserving public attention. Instead, it allows elites, as Claus Mueller has extensively argued, to interpret the diffuse grievances of the lower classes *for* them, in ways that best serve elite interests.[24]

The socialization of the Brazilian lower classes is no exception to the rule. Lower-class parents socialize their offspring into passivity and conformity to external authority. Coupled with their underdeveloped cognitive skills, this conformity makes lower-class children highly vulnerable to the authoritarian values diffused by elites through primary schools (civic education), the church, and the media.[25]

INTERNALIZATION AS ADAPTATION TO POWERLESSNESS

It would seem, then, that in human societies—that is, in highly unequal societies—indoctrination occurs more or less automatically. The structure of such societies greatly favors the ideological supremacy of the privileged, whose values lower-class parents from generation to generation normally transmit to their children. This generational transmission, however, hardly explains why lower classes accept the values of dominant groups. To say that the underprivileged accept such values because their parents did, and that their parents accepted them because their grandparents did, and so on in infinite regression, hardly constitutes an explanation of why the underprivileged accept upper-class values as their own. We need to know what it is about inequality that favors such acceptance in the first place.

The answer appears to be that the internalization of upper-class values by the underprivileged is a psychological adaptation to inequality and powerlessness. The fear of punishment and material deprivation can, over time, lead the powerless to absorb the values of the powerful in at least two different ways. In the first place, the fear of negative sanctions induces habitual compliance. Fear turns the powerless into fast learners, eager to please the powerful. Although at first they may behave in those ways without internalizing elite values, the discrepancy between their actions and their values may prove so uncomfortable a dissonance as to provide a powerful incentive for their internalization of dominant values.

Secondly, the powerless may adjust to fear and anxiety by escaping their subjective sense of powerlessness. They cannot escape their objective condition, but they can minimize their feelings of helplessness. They can do so by persuading themselves of the ultimate benevolence of power holders. The powerless, as Dennis Wrong remarked, "are inescapably subject to a will to believe in the ultimate benevolence of the power holder, in his acceptance in the last analysis of some limits to what he will demand or inflict upon them, grounded in at least a residual concern for their interests."[26] To escape their painful condition, the powerless have a need to believe that, no matter how arbitrary or capricious power holders are, their power "is part of a larger cosmos in which the power subject also has a secure place and from which he derives actual or prospective benefits."[27] Hence, the underprivileged will tend to accept the justifications of the powerful and internalize the values undergirding them to escape their subjective sense of powerlessness.

This acceptance is analogous to that of children who need to see their powerful parents as benevolent figures and to accept the punishment they suffer at their hands—no matter how cruel and unjust—as ultimately deserved and just. Anna Freud saw this acceptance as the mechanism of defense she labeled "identification with the aggressor."[28] In the presence of an all-powerful parent, the child's only defense is to reduce his subjective sense of powerlessness by becoming as much as possible like his parent: transforming "himself from the person threatened into the person who makes the threat."[29]

The most startling evidence of internalization as an adaptation to powerlessness comes from the concentration camp and the plantation system. Testimonies and studies of life in German concentration camps indicate that inmates ultimately adjusted to complete powerlessness by identifying with their captors and, to some extent, by internalizing their values.[30] Many prisoners admitted they liked to look and act like the guards. They would arrange their uniforms to make them look like those of the SS, and they shared the attitude of the SS toward the "unfit" prisoners, that is, toward the inmates who could not adjust to camp life. The survivors who had adjusted, the "older" prisoners, were instrumental in getting rid of the "unfit" and in enforcing rules, even when these were nonsensical and had long been forgotten by the SS. Their identification went so far as to lead them—even Jews themselves—to adopt the strong nationalism and antisemitism of the guards.

Similarly, there is some indication that plantation slaves also internalized the values of their masters. Stanley Elkins has argued that the concentration camp is a "special and highly perverted instance of human slavery."[31] Just as camp inmates adjusted to their powerlessness by internalizing the values of the SS, plantation slaves adjusted to theirs by internalizing those of their masters. The typical slave characterized by southern lore as Sambo was in fact docile, humble, loyal, and childlike, just as his master wanted him to be. Sambo was no mere stereotype. He reflected an internalization by the slave of the norms of behavior laid out by the master that ultimately legitimated the master's absolute power over the slave.

According to students of concentration camps and plantation slavery, this identification with the captor, and the internalization of his values, was the result of the extreme dependence of the camp inmate on the SS guard and that of the slave on his master.[32] Inmates of concentration camps, for instance, were so dependent on their guards as to have to ask permission even to defecate.[33] This childlike dependence furthered the infantilization of inmates, which in turn increased their susceptibility to identification with their aggressor. Like a child responding to the absolute power of a cruel father, the infantilized inmate adjusted to the absolute power of the SS guard by identifying with him and by internalizing the norms of behavior laid out by the SS.[34]

The behavior of camp inmates and plantation slaves is a powerful illustration of internalization as a psychological adaptation to powerlessness. The situation of inmates and slaves was one of *extreme* powerlessness. As such it brings into full view the strength of the psychological pressures pushing the powerless toward internalizing the values of the powerful. But the experience of inmates and slaves should not blind us to the pressures experienced by the powerless in less extreme situations. Even in democratic societies, the socially deprived experience pressures, though certainly of lesser intensity, to internalize the values of dominant groups. Given the inequalities of capitalist democracies, the subordinate classes are bound to experience continual defeat and frustration in their attempts to improve their lot through legitimate democratic channels. As we have noted, dominant elites are in a position to use a variety of mechanisms to suppress or reject the threatening demands of the underprivileged. As a result of their impotence to change their situation, the socially deprived experience a heightened sense of powerlessness that may take the form of intense self-deprecation.[35] From there to an internalization of the dominant belief that the powerless deserve their fate is a very short distance indeed. In this sense, internalization may also be the result of an adaptation to the difficulty of improving one's lot through democratic institutions, that is, to powerlessness in the relatively coercion-free environment of capitalist democracy. Even in democracies, the underprivileged escape their subjective sense of powerlessness, if not its objective condition, by internalizing the values of the dominant classes. There is some evidence that blacks and other socially deprived groups in America adapt to powerlessness in precisely that way.[36]

All of this suggests that the relation between coercion and legitimacy is far more subtle than is usually thought. Because it is normally assumed that consent arises out of one's free will, consent is usually conceived of as the opposite of coercion.

However, if consent is the result of a process of adaptation to powerlessness, it ultimately rests on the threat of coercion where inequality prevails.

Of course, dominant elites can facilitate adaptation by making it easier for the powerless to believe in their ultimate benevolence. Elites can help the underprivileged escape their sense of powerlessness by showing unequivocally that they, the elites, can rule by force but choose not to do so. They can show this by ruthlessly punishing rebels, on the one hand, and generously rewarding conformists, on the other. By offering symbolic rewards and some material benefits when they clearly have the power to do otherwise, dominant elites can gain strong loyalties among the underprivileged because they meet their strong psychological need to believe in the benevolence of the powerful. To be sure, the benefits themselves can go a long way in generating loyalty, but the loyalty thus generated is often far greater than that warranted by the benefits, and also tends to outlast them precisely because the benefits are mostly of symbolic value. They allow the underprivileged to believe in the benevolence of the powerful and therefore facilitate their adaptation to powerlessness.

As we shall see, the Brazilian state elites of the thirties led by Vargas were able to diffuse their authoritarian ideology and generate much loyalty among workers because they unambiguously showed them that they chose benevolence over coercion. By granting privileges and benefits to Brazilian workers, who had been previously badly mistreated, the authoritarian state elites of the thirties led workers to identify with them and to gradually internalize the view of the state as their benefactor, a view central to the authoritarian-corporative state ideology.

THE STRUGGLE TO MAINTAIN IDEOLOGICAL SUPREMACY

Even though in highly unequal societies the pressures pushing the disadvantaged to internalize dominant values are much stronger than those operating on them to reject such values, the latter are by no means insignificant. Even where authority is completely accepted, it will be the object of considerable hostility. If, on the one hand, authority is a source of security, on the other hand, it always imposes a degree of restraint. No matter how legitimate, it thus always generates some degree of frustration and resentment. As Barrington Moore has remarked, human beings are essentially ambivalent toward authority; they "always want authority at the same time that they reject and distrust it."[37] Therefore, though power holders have a great advantage in the indoctrination of the underprivileged, they will always have to guard themselves from their resentment. That is why indoctrination is usually complemented by other mechanisms, the function of which is to prevent the underprivileged from learning interpretations of reality and modes of action that are contrary to the interests of established elites. Since the socially deprived can either be taught alternative values by counterelites or learn them on their own, power holders use two corresponding preventive mechanisms. I shall refer to the first—that which is designed to prevent counterelites from teaching alternative values to the underprivileged—as *ideological insulation*. The second, designed to prevent the disadvantaged from learning alternative values on their own, involves *discouraging autonomous political participation*.

Ideological Insulation

As its label indicates, this mechanism operates to insulate the underprivileged from the influence of threatening leaders and their threatening ideas. The most extreme use of this mechanism occurs when a group of persons is torn away from its environment and thrown into a completely isolated, closed setting such as a camp, a prison, or a plantation. The complete isolation of those settings not only facilitates indoctrination but also precludes change after indoctrination has occurred. Alternatively, extreme ideological insulation can be achieved by incarcerating the opponents of dominant elites rather than the underprivileged, that is, by incarcerating the transmitters of undesirable ideas rather than the targets of indoctrination. This is, of course, a preferable strategy when the target group is too large to be isolated in a camp or a prison. That is why in autocratic societies insulation is achieved by incarcerating dissenters and censoring the means of communication rather than by isolating the great majority of the population. Of course, if one takes the world as a unit, rather than the nation-state, then autocratic societies can be thought of as camps that insulate their populations from the influence of democratic ideas.

Needless to say, incarceration and censorship are not the main means by which democratic societies achieve the ideological insulation of the underprivileged. Nevertheless, achieve ideological insulation they do, though to a lesser extent and by very different means than autocratic societies. In democratic societies, socially deprived groups are prevented from learning ideas that are critical of capitalist democracy through the deployment of economic power. Although rebels are free to express their ideas, the economic power of dominant elites prevents them from reaching the citizenry.[38] After all, most of the means of communication are privately owned. The media do not only represent business, they *are* big business. It is only natural therefore that messages against the free enterprise system should not be diffused through most of the mass media of capitalist democracy. Furthermore, even when those who manage the means of communication are tempted to allow critical ideas to be diffused, the threat of withdrawal of money for advertisement will be sufficient to prevent them from doing so.

As for the publicly owned media, they too tend to conform. Public officials also have an incentive to respect the fundamental interests of businessmen. Their welfare depends on the state of the economy, which in turn depends on private investment in a free enterprise market system. Thus, the consequent intensity of official pressures is likely to engender a conformist behavior from the publicly owned media. This does not mean that government and public officials will not be criticized. It only means that criticism will remain narrow and therefore "safe" from the point of view of dominant elites.

A third way by which dominant elites can insulate the lower

classes from undesirable potential leaders and their critical ideas is to organize them in official or semiofficial organizations before they can organize themselves or be organized by counterelites. These official or semiofficial unions and political associations are given a variety of privileges, including a monopoly of representation. In this way, established elites can isolate counterelites without resorting to force. Since the official organizations are given great advantages, they will preempt the organization of the lower classes by autonomous leaders and by counterelites. These will therefore have to penetrate the official organizations to reach the lower classes. But, as we shall see, it is fairly easy to prevent them from doing so.

Because freedom of association is a norm of democratic polities, they usually do not resort to official organizations. But, again, economic power can be used to favor moderate working-class organizations and to weaken more radical ones. Employers can help a great deal in helping moderate unions prevail against more radical ones, and businessmen can certainly help moderate parties prevail over radical ones in electoral competition. Moreover, the logic of electoral competition itself induces radical parties to increasingly move toward the center of the ideological spectrum.[39] Unless they move toward the center, they cannot accumulate enough votes to gain access to the major centers of power. As these parties become more moderate, however, they cease to be a potential source of diffusion of counterideologies among the lower classes. Thus, although dominant elites of democratic societies cannot create official organizations for the lower classes, they can nevertheless use their varied resources to see that a majority among them are organized in ways that minimize the influence of leaders and organizations that are frankly critical of capitalist democratic institutions.

It should be added that the aspects of lower-class socialization mentioned in the previous section facilitate the ideological insulation of those classes. The limited cognitive and linguistic skills that ensue from the deprived environment of the lower classes narrow their capacity to think critically about the structure of the society in which they live. Members of the lower classes are therefore often unable to understand the criticism of counterelites; their cognitive limitations seal them off from alternative interpretations of reality. Thus, even if the underprivileged are uneasy about dominant beliefs and are somewhat critical about their political environment, they are often unable to develop an alternative critical way of thinking about their world. They are likely to remain confused, or to hold contradictory ideas, or to be afflicted by what David Garson has described as "multiple consciousness," that is, by "ambiguity and overlays of consciousness" that make them extremely vulnerable to manipulation by dominant elites.[40] This is the case because, as we saw, the disadvantaged are trained to rely on authority figures. Confronted by confusion, they will thus be more likely to follow power holders than those who criticize them. Routine socialization in this way automatically provides much of the ideological insulation of the lower classes.

Discouraging Autonomous Political Participation

Even when insulated from counterelites and counterideologies, the disadvantaged may gradually develop a critical consciousness of their social and political environment through their own autonomous political organization and participation. If the lower classes are able to organize on their own to struggle for a gradual improvement of their situation, they may become increasingly aware of the limits of the benevolence of power holders as well as of the ways in which the social order is rigged against them. Democratic theorists, political scientists, sociologists, and psychologists have all argued that autonomous political participation increases political awareness and knowledge.[41] Empirical studies on political learning confirm their argument. These studies have shown that persons who participate less are also more likely to feel powerless and less likely to learn about their political environment.[42] Consequently, dominant elites wittingly or unwittingly often create and maintain institutional arrangements that are biased against the political participation of the lower classes, especially that of an autonomous kind, in order to prevent them from learning more about the causes of their situation and about the ways in which it could be changed.

Obviously, force can be used to prevent the disadvantaged from engaging in political action. But, as we have seen, force is by no means required to discourage participation. All of the mechanisms used in democratic societies to suppress threatening demands before they even reach decision-making arenas—positive and negative sanctions, the invocation of biases of the system, and the reshaping or strengthening of the mobilization of bias—are also mechanisms that discourage participation. In the long run, they persuade the underprivileged that it is not even worth trying to participate. And even when the underprivileged are able to overcome the barriers raised by these mechanisms, and with great difficulty muster the resources necessary to bring their demands into decision-making arenas, they are likely to be defeated more often than not.

In any event, inequality itself, as well as its effects on lower-class families and socialization, are natural automatic deterrents of political participation. Empirical studies on participation have shown over and over again that the lower classes participate considerably less not only because they have less of the essential resources—time, money, and skills—to do so but also because they are not taught the civic attitudes that motivate people to participate.[43] Rather, the experience of continual defeat is likely to lead the disadvantaged to teach apathy, fatalism, and resignation to their children. Consequently, as they grow older most members of the lower classes will continue to learn little about their political environment and to be highly susceptible to indoctrination by established elites. Even though the disadvantaged have much legal latitude to participate in capitalist democracies, the highly unequal character of such societies is in and of itself a potent inhibitor of autonomous political participation by the disadvantaged.

Another way of preventing autonomous participation is to preempt it by enclosing the socially deprived in organizations controlled by dominant elites. This can be done in the same way this tactic is used to ideologically insulate the lower classes, that is, either by creating official organizations that can easily overshadow autonomous ones or by giving enormous advantages to the organizations that follow a course of action that best suits the interests of the dominant elites. By enclosing the socially deprived in such official, semiofficial, or "favored" organizations, dominant elites can preempt autonomous participation and channel action in ways that reinforce the beliefs and values they instill in the lower classes. Since the method of enclosing the disadvantaged in organizations controlled by power holders can also be used for ideological insulation, it is an extremely powerful preventive mechanism—for it does double duty in preventing the disadvantaged from learning alternative beliefs and values: it prevents them both from being taught by counterelites and from learning on their own.

As we shall see in the next chapter, by creating the official corporative labor organizations through which workers participate to this day, Brazilian state elites of the thirties were using the powerful mechanism just described. By enclosing workers in official organizations, in one stroke those elites insulated workers from counterelites and counterideologies and preempted their autonomous political participation. So powerful was this effect of corporative labor organizations that they managed to maintain the beliefs and values of the authoritarian ideology even in the face of the challenges of the twenty years of democracy that followed their establishment during the dictatorship of the Estado Novo.

Chapter 6

MAINTAINING THE STATE IDEOLOGY

IT IS HARDLY surprising that Brazilian workers should have been persuaded of the benevolence of the authoritarian state elite of the Estado Novo. At the time, most workers were of recent rural origin, and the paternalism of the new authoritarian state elite was far more compatible with their traditional values than the liberalism of the older elite of the Old Republic (1899–1930). Whereas the state elite that seized power in the thirties and later formed the Estado Novo (1937–45) extended and enforced rights that improved considerably the conditions of working-class life, their predecessors, who had a marked laissez-faire orientation, had abandoned workers to their own fate. It is therefore only natural that most workers should have preferred the authoritarian paternalism of the Estado Novo to the liberalism of the Old Republic, which was foreign to them and which also seemed so hostile to workers.

Much harder to understand is why workers continued to hold the authoritarian-corporative values of the state ideology throughout the democratic regime (1945–64) that followed the Estado Novo. Once they had been organized and fully protected by the labor legislation of the Estado Novo, they could use their newly acquired democratic rights to increase their power and further improve the material conditions of their lives. One would have expected them eventually to realize that democratic institutions were at least instrumentally valuable to workers. They should have learned at least that democracy afforded them the opportunity to expand their political participation and, through it, their capacity to redress their grievances and improve their lot. Yet, as we saw, most Brazilian workers were almost unaffected by democratic institutions; they continued to hold the values and beliefs of the state ideology instilled in them by the state elites of the thirties.

In the following pages I will argue that Brazilian workers continued to hold authoritarian-corporative values because the corporative state structures created by the state elite of the thirties remained intact throughout the democratic regime. The mechanisms built into the corporative institutions preventing workers from learning alternative beliefs were sturdy enough to maintain the state ideology among workers, even in the face of strong contrary pressures from electoral institutions. Corporative institutions turned out to be effective mechanisms of power that not only facilitated the indoctrination of workers by authoritarian elites but also greatly contributed to the ideological insulation of workers and prevented their autonomous political participation. The survival of these institutions during the democratic regime therefore prevented workers from learning the more democratic values of the counterelites and from developing their own point of view through more autonomous forms of political participation.

Although the tensions between democratic and corporative institutions were not so great as to provoke a breakdown of the ideological insulation of workers, they did nevertheless undermine it a little. The corporative institutions were better able to insulate workers in the authoritarian context of the Estado Novo than they were in that of the democratic regime that followed. As we shall see, during the democratic period, counterelites managed to gain some control over the corporative system and attempted to change it from within. But they could reach only a minority of workers. Before the movement for a more autonomous working class could spread, the military intervened.

ENCLOSING THE WORKING CLASS WITH CORPORATIVE STRUCTURES

The state elite that seized the state apparatus with the Revolution of 1930 vigorously led Brazil through its most radical transformation. Under the leadership of Vargas, that state elite transformed the country from a loose federation of states ruled by rural oligarchies into a highly centralized national state that curbed even the power of the great landowners. The minimal laissez-faire state of the First Republic was changed into a strong interventionist state, which regulated a wide range of social and economic activities, directly participated in the economy, and became the major force propelling Brazil into the industrial era. As a central part of their interventionist project, the state elite of the thirties also stepped in to regulate the hitherto almost completely neglected area of labor relations.

Before 1930, urban workers had almost no legal protection.[1] It was only after World War I, when Brazil became a signatory of the International Labor Charter, that labor legislation became a more serious issue in the Congress.[2] The general strike of 1917 also helped put labor legislation on the agenda, and from then on there was a greater effort to provide some protection for the working class.[3] But the legislation that was passed was mostly restricted to the protection of women and minors, and even then it was rarely enforced.[4] There were no official organizational structures specifically designed to enforce labor laws; this task was left to the local police.[5]

The police, however, had a better record of repressing workers than of protecting their legal rights. Before 1930, the incipient labor movement of the time was led by immigrant workers of Spanish and Italian origin, who were mostly anarchists, socialists, and communists.[6] These leaders headed both political and labor associations, which were mostly small, local, and organized by craft.[7] Refusing to act within and through the political system, the radical leadership preferred to negotiate directly with employers without interference from the state.

They used the threat of strike as their major weapon in pressing for the usual reductions in hours of work and for better wages, but their ultimate intention was to prepare the working class for a revolutionary overthrow of the system.

Employers and state authorities responded by repressing the labor movement.[8] Employers undermined labor associations by dealing with labor leaders and even making concessions to workers when threatened by strikes, only to fire the leaders and withdraw the concessions to workers when the threat was over. Failing this, they enlisted the police to repress strikes and to arrest or deport the leaders of labor associations. In the liberal atmosphere of the Old Republic, organized labor was seen by the authorities as interfering with private contracts between individuals. Employers could thus always count on the police to enforce the section of the penal code dealing with "crimes against the freedom of labor" as well as on the legislation specifically aimed at foreign workers, which sanctioned their arrest and deportation. That is why the director of the Textile Industry Center could happily say that "a great cordiality reigns between the Center and the state police headquarters."[9]

When Vargas seized power in 1930, organized labor was still relatively weak. In spite of the substantial growth of the urban labor force, labor organizations continued to have only a minor impact in improving the conditions of working-class life. The anarchist and socialist leadership had always been unable to mobilize and organize more than a minority of workers, and the more recent communist leaders had not fared much better. If the radical immigrant leadership had succeeded in mobilizing part of their compatriots, they certainly had not reached the large number of Brazilian workers who had recently migrated from rural areas. These workers not only had no ethnic affinity with the radical leadership but also had no skills or experience to understand their radical ideology. They were illiterate and still highly deferential toward the upper classes, and they considered urban-industrial life an improvement over the conditions of rural areas. Anarchism and socialism had little meaning to them, and therefore the labor movement was restricted to the small militant minority among immigrant workers of an already small urban labor force.[10]

As the twenties wore on, the situation grew worse for the radical leadership. The urban labor force was increasing, but the new workers were migrants from the rural areas. By the early thirties, this trend would radically alter the ethnic composition of the labor force: the majority would be native rather than from European stock.[11] To attend to the needs of this growing group of Brazilian workers, a "reformist" leadership organized labor associations that opposed both anarchists and communists. This new leadership was willing to work within the limits of the political system and had no intentions beyond obtaining immediate benefits for the working class. It was also willing to collaborate with governments that offered some protection to workers, and favored a benevolent form of state intervention even though it remained limited by the imperatives of the capitalist system. According to the communists themselves, by the mid-thirties the "reformists" were a major group within the labor movement, if not the dominant one.[12]

The twenties therefore offered state elites the opportunity to gain the loyalty of urban workers and to control the labor movement. The urban labor force was growing, but it had not yet reached the size required to become a powerful political force, and it was growing in ways that favored a moderate leadership that was willing to make an alliance with state elites. These elites could thus coopt the reformist leaders and gain the loyalty of the native workers, which were to become a majority of the working class, before a powerful autonomous movement could be formed. State elites could take advantage of the competition among radical leaders and between those and reformist ones in order to preempt, in one move, both a possible development of a different radical labor movement and the formation of an autonomous one under the leadership of the reformists. The state elite of the Old Republic was either blind to this opportunity or precluded from pursuing it by its own liberal values. The elite that took power in the thirties was neither blind nor inhibited by its ideological inclination. Under Vargas's leadership, the authoritarian state elite of the thirties seized the opportunity to control the working class by placing it under the tutelage of the state.

As soon as it seized power in 1930, the new state elite expressed its radical disagreement with the labor policy of the Old Republic. Rather than seeing the social question as a "matter for the police" and workers as disruptive elements disturbing the "social peace," the new elite saw the working class as crucial to economic development as well as a growing political force that had to be acknowledged.[13] It therefore sought to channel and control, rather than repress, the collective action of workers by meeting, rather than denying, their most basic demands.

Even before Vargas seized power by force of arms, he had already criticized his predecessor's attitude toward the social question. In a speech given on January 2, 1930, during his presidential campaign, Vargas attacked President Washington Luiz for denying the existence of a "social question."[14] He pointed to the scarcity of social legislation and to the lack of its enforcement, arguing that Brazil had not lived up to its commitment to the International Labor Organization. Among other things, he promised to provide legislation that would protect women, children, invalids, and the aged; he promised health protection and protection against accidents; he promised to extend legislation on vacations, to reduce the number of working hours, and to institute the minimum wage; and he also promised to extend retirement and social security benefits to a wide variety of workers. When Vargas seized power and became president of the Provisional Government in November 1930, he reiterated his promises and said that as part of his immediate program he would "institute a Ministry of Labor to take charge of the social question and the protection of the urban and rural worker."[15]

Vargas kept his promises. Although he was to assume full dictatorial powers only after the coup of 1937, he also had extraordinary powers before that, allowing him to pass rather voluminous social legislation. In six years, the state elite under his leadership passed nearly five times as many laws as had been passed during the four decades of the Old Republic.[16] The eight-hour workday and retirement pensions were instituted for a broad range of occupations, the legislation protecting women and children was revised, improved, and extended, and so was that concerning accidents and vacations. Workers were greatly benefited not only by this new legislation but also by the new bureaucratic agencies that were finally created to enforce it. Less than a month after his inaugural speech, Vargas created the Ministry of Labor.[17] Shortly after that, the National Department of Labor was created, it being in charge of improving working conditions and developing a system of social security. And the year of 1932 also saw the beginnings of what was to become a very complex system of adjudication of labor disputes: the first labor courts were created.[18]

All of these measures generated much working-class support for the state elite under Vargas. The relatively sudden extension of benefits to workers led them to welcome the new interventionist state. They began to see the new role of the state as an arbiter between them and their employers as beneficial to the working class. But they did not realize that they would ultimately pay a heavy price for the state's tutelage. As it extended basic benefits to workers, the new state elite was quickly enclosing them in state structures that would greatly curtail their power, would prevent them from learning about their political environment and interests, and in the end would be turned against them, without them even realizing that this was the case.

The corporative edifice in which the new state elite finally locked the working class was completed after 1937, during the dictatorship of the Estado Novo. But already in 1931, the state elite had laid the foundations of the corporative state structure. The unionization law passed in that year foreshadowed the corporative labor system of the Estado Novo.[19] If, on the one hand, this new law protected and offered a number of rights and privileges to the labor associations recognized by the state, on the other hand, it exacted a heavy price for official recognition. The unions that gained recognition could represent the economic, legal, and other interests of workers with the government through the Ministry of Labor. They were allowed to draw up labor contracts and to maintain cooperatives, placement services, mutual aid funds, schools, and health and legal services, for which they could apply for funds and subsidies from the state. Only official unions had access to labor courts, and their members could not be harassed or fired for belonging to the unions or for disagreeing with their employers. On the other hand, to be recognized by the Ministry of Labor, a labor association had to have its membership composed of two-thirds Brazilian citizens; its officials could be elected for only a year and could not be reelected; its members could not engage in political propaganda and activities; it had to present annual reports on its activities to the Ministry of Labor; and it also had to give the ministry access to membership lists and to directives on its by-laws.

These requirements obviously excluded from recognition the politically oriented anarchist and communist associations of immigrant workers. But there were still other ways in which the Ministry of Labor could exclude labor associations it considered inconvenient. The ministry recognized only one union for a given category of workers, that which had two-thirds of the category among its members. Failing this, the ministry recognized the union that had the largest membership. This meant that if the Ministry of Labor could promote a union that had more members than a union it disliked, it could exclude the one it disliked by denying it official recognition. Furthermore, the National Department of Labor had the power to depose the elected officials of a union and even dissolve it if necessary. Since many of the leftist associations did not achieve recognition, their leaders and members had no legal protection, which meant that they could be harassed by both their employers and the police. Although they were not legally prohibited, anarchist and communist labor associations were thus doubly handicapped. Not only did the law reward workers who were members of the officially recognized unions. In a rather insidious way, the state also punished workers who remained in the unofficial radical unions.

The state elite under Vargas thus gave a great advantage to the more moderate "reformist" labor leadership and gradually gained the loyalty of the majority of urban workers. In doing so, it also gained a substantial degree of control over the moderate leadership and its associations, thus preempting the formation of what could have been a powerful autonomous labor movement of a more moderate nature. In a word, the new state elite isolated the older radical labor leadership and began to enclose the working class within a corporative edifice, which was completed a decade later. Although the progressive enclosure of urban workers suffered a setback in 1934, when a more liberal unionization law was passed, it was short-lived and the labor movement never really regained the autonomy it had before 1930.[20] The authoritarian Constitution of 1937 and the unionization law of 1939 reestablished with even greater vigor the corporative organization of labor, which finally took its last form in the monumental labor code of 1943.[21]

By then, through its use of a shrewd combination of force and cooptation, the state elite of the Estado Novo had completely enclosed the Brazilian working class within the corporative state edifice and had persuaded the majority of workers of the benevolence of the authoritarian-corporative state. By granting them the protection of the state, which their liberal predecessors had so vehemently refused, the authoritarian state elite had met the majority of urban workers halfway in their traditional need to believe in the benevolence of the powerful. Brazilian workers therefore gradually internalized a preference for the corporative state, absorbing much of the state ideology diffused in deeds and words by the state elite. Their loyalty to Vargas as well as the corporative values they internalized were to show much resilience in the face of considerable social change. Urban workers fought to keep Vargas in power at the end of the Estado Novo, in 1945; they helped him regain the presidency, in 1950; they mourned him in the streets after his suicide, in 1954; and they still thought he was the greatest president Brazil ever had, as our survey showed, in 1972, nearly twenty years after his death. In 1972, workers also trusted the state as their greatest benefactor, and a crushing majority among them thought the state should actively control the unions.

THE CORPORATIVE LABOR SYSTEM AND THE MAINTENANCE OF THE STATE IDEOLOGY

Political beliefs, values, and loyalties can change, especially when major social, economic, and political changes occur, as they did in Brazil after 1945. One cannot explain their permanence merely by referring to their distant origin. It is also necessary to explain how beliefs and values are maintained in the face of pressures for change, that is, to describe the mechanisms that keep them alive in time. In the particular case of the values of Brazilian workers, it is therefore necessary to describe the mechanism that kept the state ideology alive among them during the twenty years of democracy that followed the demise of the Estado Novo in 1945.

It was the corporative labor system in the final form it took in the labor code of 1943 (Consolidação das Leis do Trabalho, or CLT) that maintained the state ideology dominant among the working class during the democratic period. Almost unaltered after 1945, it acted as a mechanism of power, preventing workers from learning other political beliefs and values.[22] Although the uneasy coexistence of representative democracy and corporative structures strained those structures, the corporative labor system was effective in performing the functions of both insulating workers ideologically and preventing their autonomous political participation.

The corporative labor system is a three-tiered structure controlled by the Ministry of Labor.[23] At the bottom are the *sindicatos,* local unions, which represent workers in one or a few *municípios,* an area roughly equivalent to a county or township. The *sindicatos* are linked at the state level in federations, which are composed of at least five *sindicatos* in the same branch of the economy and usually in the same state. The federations in turn are linked in national confederations, which are constituted of at least three federations and are directly linked to the Ministry of Labor. Whereas the federations and confederations act in the political and administrative fields, and its leaders have frequent contacts with ministry officials, the local unions deal mostly with workplace grievances and welfare services.

This corporative structure prevents counterelites from influencing workers in two different but related ways. In the first place, it prevents those elites from forming their own autonomous labor associations. Although unofficial labor organizations are not legally prohibited, they cannot survive the competition from the *sindicatos*. Within a county or township, only one labor organization is officially recognized for each of the government-specified jurisdictions, which covers all workers in "identical, similar, or connected trades." The officially recognized union, and only it, is granted legal representation of the workers within its jurisdiction. Without such recognition, a labor organization can neither legally negotiate collective contracts nor use the courts, and it is not allowed access to government administrative bodies.

Even worse, without recognition a labor organization has no access to government-guaranteed financing. Only officially recognized unions are entitled to a share of the trade-union tax *(impôsto sindical)*. This tax is collected from all workers in the union's jurisdiction whether they are union members or not. The union tax is collected in March, and it is equivalent to the remuneration the worker received for one day of work per year. About 54 percent of the total amount collected by the government returns to the *sindicato*, which constitutes 60 percent of the *sindicato* revenues.[24] Needless to say, the privileges afforded by official recognition make it almost impossible for a labor organization to survive outside the official corporative structure. Counterelites and labor leaders who are against it are thus forced to attempt to work within that structure if they are to influence workers at all.

But there is a second set of controls built into the corporative structure that act to prevent the rebellious leader from attaining influential positions within the union. Inconvenient leaders can easily be declared ineligible for elective positions. The law regulating eligibility is sufficiently vague to interpret any of a very wide range of action as disqualifying an undesirable prospective candidate. This can be clearly seen from a reading of Article 530 of the labor code:

> No one can be elected to administrative positions or positions of economic or professional representation, nor continue to exercise these duties:
>
> 1. who has not had his accounts approved while in administrative office.
> 2. who has injured the well-being of any sindical entity.
> 3. who is neither a union officer nor a worker in the activity or profession within the territorial base represented by the union.
> 4. who has been convicted of fraud, during the period of punishment.
> 5. who has lost his political rights.
> 6. who, publicly and ostensibly, through acts or words, defends the ideological principles of political parties whose registration has been canceled or of an association or entity of any type whose activities have been considered contrary to the national interest and whose registration has been canceled or whose functions have been suspended by competent authorities.
> 7. who is guilty of proven bad conduct.
> 8. who has been removed from administrative office or sindical representation.[25]

Another way to control recalcitrant leaders is to freeze the union's account in the Bank of Brazil, which is responsible for transferring the part of the union tax due to the *sindicato.* Government officials can do so by invoking Article 592 of the labor code.[26] According to this article, the union tax can be used only for job placement; for maternity, medical, dental, and legal assistance; for professional and vocational training schools; for credit and consumer cooperatives; for vacation facilities, libraries, social and sporting activities, and funeral aid; and for expenses incurred in the administration of the above activities. The tax revenues cannot be used as strike funds or for other militant activities. If the government decides that the tax has been misused, which it can do very easily, the union's account is frozen by the Bank of Brazil. In addition, officials can also bar a leader's access to government administrative bodies that control large sources of patronage, such as the social security institutes, thus crippling his ability to secure benefits for his union's members and putting a damper on his popularity.

Failing all of these sanctions, the Ministry of Labor can use its right to intervene in the *sindicato* or cancel its recognition. The right of intervention allows the ministry to seize union headquarters and funds and appoint a delegate or junta to administer the *sindicato*. In theory, intervention is supposed to occur only when there is internal conflict within the union or other problems that prevent its normal operation. In practice, however, it is very easy for the government to find a pretext to intervene, for, as Erickson remarks, "internal squabbling and errors on the books—intentional or accidental—almost always exist."[27] Canceling the union's recognition is not used as much because it implies eliminating the welfare services of the *sindicato*. This can create a great deal of discontent among workers, because the services provided by the social security institutes are poor and insufficient.

State elites discourage rebellious behavior by not only controlling union elections, withdrawing funds from union coffers, and intervening in their operations. They also encourage conformity to corporative norms by rewarding well-behaved leaders in generous ways. The unions provide little opportunity for upward mobility. A union officer can receive a salary only if his position forces him to be absent from his regular job, and even then he cannot get more than what he usually receives from his regular job. The labor law also limits the number of paid union officers to seven, regardless of the size of the union. As Kenneth Mericle notes, the "law is clearly designed to prevent union leaders from using union revenues to create an independent power base within the union or to promote their own social and economic mobility."[28] On the other hand, the union leader is offered an opportunity for upward mobility outside the union structure, but it is strictly controlled by the government.

If the labor leader is cooperative, he can get one of the many positions as a labor judge in the lower-level labor courts. The court system has three levels. At the first level are the conciliation courts *(juntas de conciliação e julgamento)*, where individual grievances are resolved. The second level consists of the regional labor courts *(tribunals regionais do trabalho)*, where individual grievances are appealed and wages are set. The third level is the supreme labor court, which is the court of appeal for the regional labor courts. At all three levels, the courts are tripartite bodies consisting of one government-appointed professional judge, one employer delegate, and one labor delegate, but the positions in the lower-level courts are the most numerous. In each major population center, there is at least one such lower-level court, and in the very large centers such as São Paulo there are as many as thirty-two, each requiring one labor judge and one substitute.[29] These are chosen from lists of *sindicato* nominees by the president of the Regional Labor Court, who is a government-appointed court official.

The government-controlled labor court positions are very valuable because they require little time and attention yet can command salaries as high as ten times or more the minimum wage. In addition to positions in the labor courts, there are many attractive government-controlled positions in the vast number of permanent commissions in the Ministry of Labor that require an equal representation of workers and employers and in the considerable number of tripartite bodies in the social security bureaucracy. All of these offer very lucrative positions for the cooperative labor leader.[30]

It is no wonder therefore that the corporative labor structure insulates urban workers both from leftist leaders and from the more moderate ones who want to create an autonomous labor movement during the democratic regime. The peculiar mix of inducements and constraints of the corporative structure effectively prevents those rebellious leaders from either creating autonomous associations outside the official structure or influencing workers within that structure. Instead, it effectively maintains docile labor leaders at the head of the corporative structures who perpetuate among workers the norms of behavior, beliefs, and values prescribed by the state ideology. But that is not all.

The corporative labor structure also prevents workers from learning alternative beliefs because it contains mechanisms that inhibit the participation of workers. The organic-statist labor code encourages collaboration and conciliation, the duties of the *sindicato* being "to collaborate with the public authorities in the development of social solidarity" and "to promote conciliation in labor disputes."[31] It therefore discourages militant activity of any sort. Only very few types of strikes are considered legal, and workers cannot strike without previous authorization from the regional labor court. Unauthorized strikes can be punished by suspending or firing workers, removing leaders from office, imposing fines on the union, freezing its accounts, and even cancelling the union's registration.[32] Government officials and the courts usually try to settle disputes between workers and employers either informally or through the courts; strikes are avoided as much as possible. The coopted union leaders cooperate in avoiding strikes and other political activities. They strive to maintain the union as a mere bureaucratic welfare agency of the state and to keep workers as passive as possible.

Finally, it should be noted that the structure of the official corporative system itself curtails the collective action of workers and minimizes their power to influence government policy. *Sindicatos* are prevented from having direct horizontal links with each other; they have no formal link with each other. The unions are linked only vertically, through the federations, which means that broad and united working-class actions can be coordinated only through the federations. But these are tightly controlled by government officials, who can control elections for federation and confederation leaders. The possibility of large-scale collective action on the part of workers is thus highly dependent on government officials.[33]

Thus deprived of autonomous collective action and insulated from counterelites, urban workers have continued to hold the authoritarian-corporative beliefs and values that form the core of the state ideology. Most of them have never had the opportunity to learn about alternative ways of organizing relations between workers, employers, and the state. The majority of workers have never learned about autonomous unions and how they could help them increase their power and improve their situation. Surveys of working-class attitudes toward unions and the state show that, throughout the democratic period, the majority of workers continued to think of unions as welfare agencies of the state.[34] Because they assumed the state is benevolent, urban workers neither saw any need for militant action nor understood that the corporative system is rigged against them. Because the co-opted leaders and the corporative unions discourage collective action directed at improving the material conditions of workers, these could not learn how more militant unions would have improved their situation. By the same token, they could not see how corporative unions were used to control their wages and to preempt the formation of a more powerful working class.

As for the more rebellious leaders, they were either prevented from reaching workers or unable to persuade the workers that the state is not really benevolent. Because they were prevented from acting against the state, militant leaders were unable to demonstrate to workers that alternative forms of organization would have better served their interests. There is evidence showing that most workers did not understand the militant leaders.[35] They did not understand what an autonomous organization of state-union relations implies, nor did they understand why they should be against corporative unions. Most did not see the link between the corporative welfare union and the politico-economic control of the working class.

If the majority of workers continued to hold the beliefs and values of the state ideology, it is nevertheless likely that at least some workers were changed by democratic politics. As we shall now see, democratic institutions began to erode the corporative system in the fifties. Before the effect of democratic institutions could spread, however, the military intervened.

DEMOCRACY AND THE EROSION OF THE CORPORATIVE SYSTEM

Democratic institutions had only a minor impact on the corporative system because the democratic system was largely shaped by the state elite of the Estado Novo.[36] Vargas and his followers were able to shape the electoral system and the party system of the democratic regime established in 1945. They did so in a way that integrated democratic and corporative institutions as much as possible, which allowed them a great deal of control over the political process throughout most of the democratic period. In spite of this, the democratic process did make inroads in the corporative system toward the end of that period.

Shortly before the end of World War II, the elite that controlled the state apparatus of the Estado Novo realized that their semifascist regime would be in trouble with the coming demise of fascism in Europe.[37] Anticipating future problems, the political elite of the Estado Novo realized that, rather than resisting change, it stood to gain from taking the lead in transforming their dictatorship into a democratic regime. The men who ran the Estado Novo knew that, if they granted democratic rights peacefully, they could use the resources of the state under their control to maintain the structure of power of the old regime even after formal democratic institutions had been introduced. Led by Vargas, the political elite of the Estado Novo therefore promised, in 1943, a return to democracy after the war. In this way, they could reach a compromise with the alienated members of the elite who were pressing for a democratization of the political system.[38] This compromise gave the dominant elite much leeway in preparing itself for competition in the forthcoming regime.

The state elite of the Estado Novo had greatly expanded the power of central government over the old state oligarchies and over urban workers, whom, as we saw, it had controlled through the corporative institutions. During the relatively peaceful transition to democracy, between 1943 and 1945, it used the resources of this geatly expanded state to forge the broad electoral coalition that would allow it to perpetuate its power in the future regime. In preparation for electoral competition, the men who ran the powerful bureaucracies of the Estado Novo in the states used them to organize the Social Democratic Party (PSD). Those who ran the Estado Novo's corporative labor structure, through which the state controlled the working class, used it to form the Labor Party (PTB). By bringing these two groups together, the political elite of the old regime forged the broad class coalition underlying the electoral alliance between the PSD and the PTB, which allowed it to perpetuate its power throughout the democratic period.[39]

Since this alliance was dominant during the democratic regime, the Vargas elite was able to reproduce at the political level what it had achieved at the level of labor relations. The Labor Party (PTB) created by Vargas preempted the formation of a more genuine and autonomous working-class party much in the same way that the corporative system preempted the formation of a more genuine and autonomous labor movement.[40] Since the Communist Party was banned in 1947, even the extreme left had to work side by side with the more moderate opposition from within the Labor Party and the corporative structure.[41] The strategy of both moderates and radicals was to infiltrate those structures in an attempt to gain sufficient control to use them for their reformist or radical purposes.

Their opportunity to do so increased after Vargas's return in the fifties. Vargas's nationalist policy of development required the active support of the more militant politicians and labor leaders within the Labor Party and the corporative system.[42] In exchange for their support, Vargas relaxed the control of the Ministry of Labor over the unions. The labor law was not strictly applied, interunion coordination bodies were formed, and the frequency of strikes increased.[43]

The relaxation of corporative controls gave the moderate and the radical left an opportunity to increase their power within the corporative labor structures; this power was again greatly enhanced with the passage of the Social Security Act of 1960.[44] Prior to the act, the social security system was composed of institutes formed along sectoral lines roughly parallel to those of the *sindicato* system. These institutes were administered by state-appointed technicians and experts, and they were an important source of patronage both in terms of the number of jobs and in terms of the scarce services they provided. Workers who wanted access to medical institutions or to other agencies dispensing welfare services had to get the assistance of labor leaders with contacts in the social security system. In exchange, leaders could get their vote or their participation in strikes or demonstrations. Thus, when the Act of 1960 transformed the institutes into tripartite bodies giving labor leaders one-third of the seats on the governing councils of all the social security agencies, it substantially expanded their power in the corporative system.

As long as the new positions created by the Act of 1960 were occupied mostly by docile labor leaders, control over labor remained in the hands of the government. But when Goulart made Almino Alfonso his Labor minister in 1963 in order to maintain his support at the nationalist left, radical labor leaders were able to gain a great deal of control over the corporative system.[45] As Erickson has shown, Almino Alfonso not only succeeded in placing radical labor leaders in the social security system but also "in replacing a number of moderate government representatives on the social security councils with radical nationalists who would vote with the delegates of labor."[46]

By the early sixties, the several groupings at the left had gained a great deal of control over the corporative labor system. But instead of changing the system, they used it to influence government policy. Instead of attempting to create an autonomous labor movement and to persuade workers of its advantages, they used their organizational power to channel the material grievances of workers toward the pursuit of their own radical ends, that is, toward major transformations of the politico-economic system. But, as they soon were to discover, the radical leaders could not seize power and implement major changes merely by conquering top positions within the corporative structure and opportunistically using the economic grievances of workers to destabilize the political system.[47] They had achieved some influence over the government, but, as John Humphrey has put it, they had done so within the corporative structure, "reproducing the top-heavy bureaucratic model that had been developed by Vargas in the Estado Novo period."[48] They had thus neglected the establishment of a solid rank-and-file base and were thus extremely vulnerable to a right-wing offensive. Although they had partially broken through the walls of insulation of the corporative system and had initiated much autonomous collective action, the militant union leaders had used their newly gained power neither to change workers' beliefs and values nor to restructure the corporative system. When the military intervened in 1964, the corporative labor system was still in place, and the majority of workers continued to see things as they had always seen them—through the veil of the state ideology.

Chapter 7

THE FUTURE OF THE STATE IDEOLOGY

MILITANT LABOR leaders had to wait more than ten years after the coup for another chance to challenge the corporative labor system. They had to wait until President Geisel decided to promote a liberalization of the military regime in 1974. Just as the democratization of Brazil in 1946 allowed radical labor leaders to break through the insulating barriers of the official labor structure, the liberalization of the military regime in 1974 allowed militant labor leaders to again mobilize part of the working class in an effort to attain greater freedom for labor organizations. The labor leaders of the seventies, however, adopted an entirely different strategy. Whereas the radical leaders of the sixties attempted to transform the corporative system (as well as the rest of Brazilian society) from above, the militant labor leaders of the seventies attempted to transform it from below.

The radical labor leaders of the sixties had sought to gain control of the top positions within the corporative labor structure in order to use the corporative state structures to radically transform Brazilian society. They were part of a broader movement that attempted to work from within the state in order to transform, from above, both the character of the state itself and that of society as well. After 1964, however, the attainment of such broad political ends, and the strategy they informed, were both out of the question.

After the military coup, militant leaders could no longer hope to transform the whole politico-economic system, much less from above. Faced with a hostile state, they could no longer work through it. If they wanted to improve the conditions of workers under the military regime, labor leaders had to pursue far more modest apolitical goals and to work from below, with as much independence from the state as they possibly could. That is exactly what was done by a group of labor leaders from the most modern sector of the Brazilian economy—the southern São Paulo industrial belt, especially the automobile industry of São Bernardo do Campo.

The new "authentic" labor leadership that emerged after the coup focused strictly on union matters and on the immediate interests of workers. Their strategy was to organize the rank-and-file in the plants and pressure employers directly, rather than through the state and its corporative channels. By engaging workers in autonomous collective action to improve their wages and working conditions, labor leaders hoped they could show them that the state and the corporative structures were on the side of the employers. Workers would then realize that they could improve their situation only by struggling for more autonomous labor organizations. In the longer run, perhaps such a mobilization of workers could bring about a dismantling of the corporative machinery of control.

Since an essential component of the strategy of the authentic leaders was to persuade workers that the state and its corporative structure in fact acted against their interests, and since their strategy was partially successful, the new unionism must have changed the political beliefs and values of a significant number of workers. It is tempting to speculate that many workers, at least in the modern sector, no longer believe in the core tenets of the state ideology. But it would be imprudent to say that the state ideology no longer has a future in Brazil. In spite of the country's long-awaited return to democracy in 1985, the corporative system is still very much alive.

THE LIBERALIZATION OF THE MILITARY REGIME

The liberalization of the regime came in 1974, right on the heels of its economic success. Between 1967 and 1973, a period now known as that of the "economic miracle," Brazil experienced an unprecedented combination of very high rates of growth with very low rates of inflation.[1] As table 7 shows, inflation fell at a dizzying pace after 1964. As it sank to 20 percent in 1973, the economy grew at the spectacular rate of 14 percent in the same year.

The economic success of the military regime was a mixed blessing. If on the one hand it legitimized the regime, on the other hand it ultimately alienated several elite groups that had previously supported the military, for the frenetic pace of

TABLE 7.
Inflation and Growth in Brazil, 1964 –1982

Year	*Price Increase*	*Growth in Gross Domestic Product*
1964	87.8	2.9
1965	55.4	2.7
1966	39.5	3.8
1967	28.8	4.8
1968	27.8	11.2
1969	20.3	10.0
1970	18.2	8.8
1971	17.3	13.3
1972	17.4	11.7
1973	20.5	14.0
1974	31.5	9.8
1975	32.7	5.6
1976	41.9	9.0
1977	44.1	4.7
1978	40.8	6.0
1979	77.2	6.4
1980	110.2	8.5
1981	97.0	−1.9
1982	99.7	0.0

SOURCE: Alves, *Estado e Oposição no Brasil (1964–1984)*, pp. 331, 333.

economic growth was based on an equally dizzying rate of concentration of power, which excluded from decision making elites who had been influential in the past.[2]

At least up to 1967, the military regime enjoyed much support in spite of its repressive character and the harsh measures of economic austerity it had adopted.[3] These unpopular measures were accepted as necessary to fight communism, corruption, and inefficiency, the three evils associated with the previous regime. Nevertheless, military rule was seen as a temporary necessity, never as a permanent solution. It was expected that, as communism and corruption were eradicated and the economy recuperated, the military would return power to civilians. As the military gave no sign of doing so, elites became suspicious, and opposition grew.[4]

As Peter McDonough has argued, the very success of the authoritarian regime undermined its legitimacy, because the economic miracle called into question the continued necessity of repressive policies.[5] As the country prospered, the military suffered a loss of legitimacy from which it never recuperated. Continued repression and concentration of power began to alienate the established elites who had supported the regime. Gradually, the political elite, the church, and the business community joined students, intellectuals, and labor leaders to form an ample movement for the political liberalization of the country.[6] The military responded with more repression, unleashing the most ferocious wave of repression since the coup. The period of the economic miracle was also the most repressive in terms of both the curtailment of political rights, deaths under torture, and political "disappearances."[7] (See figure 1.)

By the early seventies, however, the fight against urban guerillas and the containment of a growing unarmed opposition had swelled excessively the security apparatus of the state. The secret service apparatus had acquired a degree of autonomy from the regular military and the government, an autonomy that threatened the corporate unity of the military and its public image. Although elite groups had not yet openly and aggressively opposed the military, it also became evident that the excesses of the security apparatus had greatly contributed to the erosion of the legitimacy of the regime. Important groups within the military then felt that a gradual liberalization of the political process was necessary in order to control the security organs, to restore unity to the military, and to contain the erosion in legitimacy.[8] Thus in 1974 the Geisel government began to promote the liberalization of the regime, which would lead to a return to democracy a decade later.[9]

The liberalization of the regime brought the opposition out in the open. With the relaxation of censorship and more open elections, politicians were able to form a more genuine opposi-

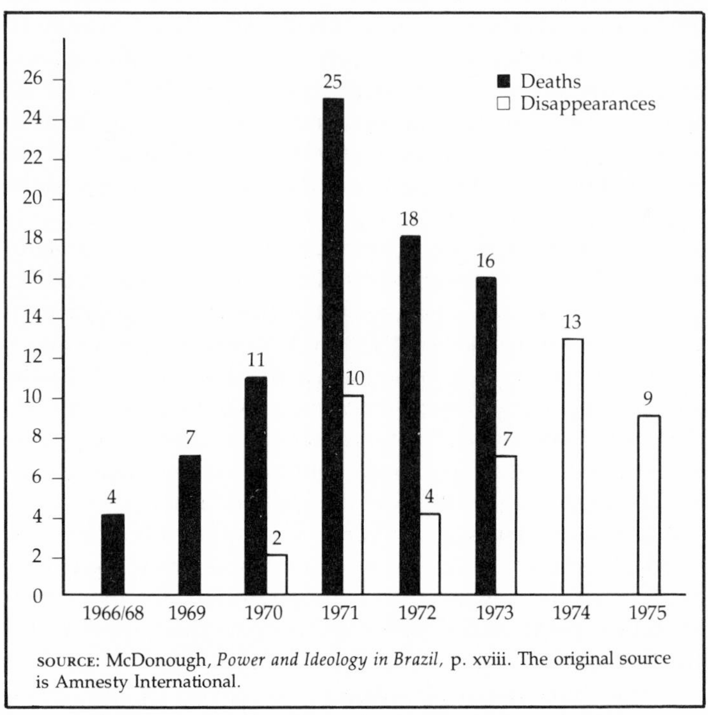

SOURCE: McDonough, *Power and Ideology in Brazil*, p. xviii. The original source is Amnesty International.

FIGURE 1. Number of Deaths under Torture and Political "Disappearances," 1966–1975

tion movement and gain major electoral victories.[10] The church became increasingly vocal against violations of human rights and expanded its activities against the security apparatus of the state.[11] In 1975 the business community joined the fray by launching its campaign against "statism," and shortly thereafter labor leaders of the dynamic sector of the economy mounted a serious working-class opposition movement against the military regime.[12]

LIBERALIZATION AND THE NEW UNIONISM

The relaxation of controls on the press, the return of public political debate and of relatively free elections, and most of all, the increasing restraint imposed on the security forces allowed the so called authentic labor leaders to pursue their strategy and expose the corporative system.[13] The labor leaders of the Metalworkers' Union of São Bernardo do Campo and Diadema were in a particularly good position to take advantage of the liberalization of the regime to mount a major challenge to the corporative system.

In the first place, the union represented a large number of workers. Between 1950 and 1960, the installation of auto plants in São Bernardo had caused a spurt of growth in its population, which grew from about 4,000 to 20,000 during those ten years.[14] Later, the economic miracle turned the area into one of the largest centers of workers in the manufacturing industry. By 1970 there were about 75,000 workers in São Bernardo.[15] Secondly, these workers the union represented were highly concentrated in a few plants. More than half of them worked in the five large auto plants of São Bernardo. And thirdly, the union could rely on a relatively high proportion of skilled workers who had greater job security, greater opportunity for movement within the plant, and a higher level of education, all of which greatly facilitated organization for collective action.

Aside from these advantages, the leaders of the Metalworkers' Union of São Bernardo could also turn to their advantage the particularly close connection between the employment policies of the auto industry and the coercive wage and job stability policies of the military. Employers in the auto industry offered considerably higher wages than those paid in other industries, though even these higher wages lagged behind the productivity increases the industry had achieved as the miracle took place. But the auto industry extracted a heavy toll from its workers.[16] They enforced a high degree of work intensity, which had a strong negative effect on health and safety in the plants. In order to keep their wage costs at a minimum, the industry also maintained a system of high rotation of labor, which virtually eliminated job security and produced much frustration and anxiety among workers.

The employment policy of the auto industry—high wages and high turnover—was made possible by the changes the military regime implemented where job stability and wage settlements were concerned.[17] In 1966, the military introduced a new law concerning job stability and compensation for dismissal. The old stability law of the Estado Novo protected workers with more than ten years of employment and made it expensive to fire workers without proving that they had commited a serious breach of discipline or responsibility. The new law (FGTS) withdrew the protection given to workers with more than ten years of service and greatly cheapened dismissal without just cause.[18]

As for wages, the military also issued in 1966 a decree transforming the wage-setting process into a purely automatic procedure. Each year, wages were to be revised according to a rigid formula applied and enforced by the labor courts. Although the labor code allowed for direct negotiation between unions and employers, in cases where one of the parties refused to negotiate or where attempts at conciliation by the regional labor office failed, the labor court would impose an agreement by compulsory arbitration. This compulsory arbitration was the standard form of collective bargaining in Brazil, and during the military regime it allowed employers of the auto industry to maintain wage increases well below increases in productivity.[19] All they had to do was to refuse to negotiate, thus imposing the automatic increases permitted by the new wage policy—which were well below increases in productivity. Since the military had virtually banned strikes, workers were defenseless.[20] They had to accept whatever increases employers offered during the annual wage-settlement meetings.

The close connection between the employment policies of the auto industry and the wage and job stability policies of the military offered a unique opportunity to expose the corporative labor system as inimical to the interests of workers. It made it easier to show to workers in the auto industry that they could no longer hope to improve their situation through the official labor institutions. It would follow that they had to pressure employers directly. Should they do so and win concessions from employers, workers would then learn that direct negotiation unfettered by the corporative machinery of the state was to their advantage. The risk was, of course, that before workers could gain any benefits from direct pressure, the military government would intervene in favor of the employers. Nevertheless, if the government intervened it would have to claim that it was enforcing the corporative labor laws, and this would have shown workers that the corporative system was against their interests. Whatever the outcome, then, by engaging workers in the auto industry in a struggle to improve their wages and working conditions, the labor leadership could show that, far from being a paternalistic arbiter, the state was on the side of the employers. The labor leaders of the Metalworkers' Union of São Bernardo thus had a unique opportunity to turn the repressive policies of the military regime to their advantage and to seriously challenge the corporative labor system.

VICTORIES AND DEFEATS OF THE NEW UNIONISM

In spite of their advantages and opportunities, there was not much the militant labor leadership of the modern sector could do before the liberalization of 1974. The great majority of their constituency was still unmobilized, and to attempt any major action in the repressive atmosphere of the Médici government

(1969–74) would have imperiled the whole authentic movement.[21] At most, the leadership could try to quietly organize workers within the plants and prepare for action at a later time.

The time to make the first major effort to discredit the corporative system came in 1977, when the Federation of Metalworkers challenged the federal government in court. The federation, which represented thirty-three unions and 650,000 workers, sought to recoup the wage losses it claimed workers had suffered in 1973.[22] It claimed that, because the government had underestimated the inflation rate, workers had received smaller wage increases, which could be compensated only by a 34 percent increase. The compensation *(reposição)* campaign, however, was mostly restricted to appeals to the government, which the latter tolerated with benign neglect. Most unions did not have the means to go beyond appealing or were afraid of doing so, and their appeals fell on deaf ears.

The leaders of the Metalworkers' Union of São Barnardo took advantage of this situation to show workers that the state and its corporative structures were against them. Referring to the 1977 compensation campaign, Lula, the president of the union at the time, said:

> We talked with the workers in meetings and through the union's paper and said that the most important thing was not the 34 percent, but rather to get rid of what had caused the theft in 1973 and 1974—the lack of trade union freedom. So, by means of the struggle over the *reposição* we had a way of openly combatting the wages policy and the trade union structure and of making workers aware of the issue.[23]

The next step was to convince workers that they had to organize and negotiate the compensation directly with the employers, since the legal channels provided by the state were not solving their problems. This step was successfully taken. A large number of workers agreed to negotiate the compensation directly with the employers, and they voted to create groups in factories to help mobilize workers for possible strike action at a future date.[24] By the end of 1977, the strategy of the authentic leaders had already worked. Many metalworkers had realized that the legal channels provided by the state would not help them solve their problems. Workers realized that they had to organize in the plants and pressure employers directly.

When employers refused to compensate them, metalworkers were prepared to strike. As the wage increase produced by the 1978 wage settlement meetings was considerably lower than the one metalworkers had campaigned for, in May of that year the Metalworkers' Union of São Bernardo went on strike. The strike quickly spread to Santo André, São Caetano, Osasco, and the city of São Paulo. It is estimated that in the first four months of the strike 280,000 workers were involved and 250 firms stopped and that about 1 million workers were ultimately affected by the wage agreements that resulted from those stoppages.[25]

The strike movement of 1978 was victorious.[26] Although the regional labor court declared it illegal, which could have meant intervention in the unions and a deposition of the leaders of the strikes, the employers decided to negotiate and offered a wage increase above the officially established maximum increase. The 1978 strike was thus an unprecedented victory; it seriously questioned the corporative system and showed the advantages of direct negotiation without the interference of the state. It showed that strikes and free collective bargaining were both possible and profitable, which emboldened workers to strike again in 1979 and 1980. On those two occasions, however, the labor court declared the strikes illegal, and this time the government intervened and deposed the leadership of the unions. In 1980, the Ministry of Labor went further and prosecuted leaders under the National Security Law for their activities in the strike. And this time around, employers were much less willing to negotiate directly with the unions; they preferred to invoke the corporative legislation and called on the military government to enforce it.

Although the authentic movement has lost much of its vigor since then and has only recently (after the return to democracy in 1985) begun to recuperate its strength, it has already had a profound impact on the relations between the state, employers, and workers. As Maria H. Moreira Alves has noted, since the strikes of 1980 many large firms have allowed unions to maintain elected delegates in the factories and have been willing to negotiate directly with union leaders on an informal basis.[27] Apparently, an unofficial system of independent relations between employers and workers parallel to the corporative system is forming roots in modern Brazil.

THE NEW UNIONISM AND THE STATE IDEOLOGY

In all likelihood, the authentic trade union movement had an impact on the political consciousness of a significant number of workers in the modern sector of the economy. As we saw, the authentic leaders made a deliberate attempt to educate workers about the negative consequences of the corporative labor system. They made a constant effort to demonstrate to workers that their autonomous organization and collective action could improve their situation and that, since the state and corporative institutions inhibited such action, these institutions were against the interests of the working class. Unlike previous militant labor leaders, the authentic ones were able to reach workers and mobilize them, because they dealt with issues of immediate concern to workers—issues that workers could understand—rather than with the complex abstract political issues that were part of the leftist rhetoric of the early sixties.

Of course, the authentic labor leaders had an unprecedented opportunity to show to the workers of the modern sector that the tutelage of the state and the corporative system were not in their interest. Unlike the authoritarian elites of the Estado Novo and the populist elites of the democratic regime that followed it, the military did not act in paternalistic ways. On the contrary, the military used mainly the coercive aspects of the corporative structure and neglected its manipulative potential. In the particular context of the auto industry, the exceptionally repressive behavior of the military gave the authentic labor leaders a unique opportunity to bring out in the open the true nature of the corporative labor system.

The number and concentration of workers in the auto industry, and the high proportion of skilled workers among them, also helped the authentic leaders organize them to engage in autonomous collective action, which ultimately exposed the manipulative character of the corporative system and ideology. With the advent of liberalization, therefore, the authentic leaders were in a position to neutralize the power mechanisms of the corporative structure and fully exploit the advantages of the particular situation of their constituencies to expose the corporative labor system. It is to the credit of the authentic leaders, however, that they should have clearly seen the opportunity to expose corporative arrangements and to have used the most adequate strategy to do so.

Because the authentic leaders used such an effective strategy to mobilize workers and to engage them in autonomous action, they must have altered the beliefs of at least a significant number of workers in the modern sector. Since the strikes of the late seventies made so visible the repressive nature of the state and the manipulative character of the corporative system, it is likely that a substantial number of workers in the modern sector now doubt the benevolence of the state and other core beliefs of the state ideology. Given that democratic practices and the growth of the modern industrial sector both have a corrosive effect on corporative structures, should Brazil remain democratic, the future does not hold much promise for the state ideology.

Chapter 8

CONCLUSION

THE KEY arguments of this book are two. The first is that the power of authoritarian elites over Brazilian urban workers has been sturdier, and more subtle, than is usually assumed. I argued that, far from being based merely on naked coercion, the power of those elites has been largely based on consent. On this score, the evidence is clear. Brazilian workers espoused the authoritarian-corporative values embedded in the state ideology of political elites. They believed that a strong authoritarian state looked after their interests better than a democratic one, and they were largely contemptuous of electoral politics. They saw democratic politics not only as detrimental to their own interests but also as precluding good government and the achievement of the common good. Brazilian workers saw authoritarian-corporative governments as more orderly, honest, and efficient, and believed that only such governments could promote the public good.

The other main argument of this book concerns the origins of working-class consent. Here my argument is that such consent was engineered by the authoritarian elites of the thirties and maintained by the political elites who inherited their power. This argument was supported in two different but complementary ways. I first analyzed the situation of Brazilian workers and showed there was no reason to expect them to adopt the values of the state ideology. On the contrary, everything about their situation led us to expect them to have very different beliefs and values and to be far less passive and quiescent than they were. It was thus plausible to suspect that Brazilian elites had instilled in workers the authoritarian values of the state ideology in order to secure their quiescence and consent.

To suspect indoctrination, however, is a long way from establishing its occurrence. Further empirical support is needed. One must also describe the mechanisms by which workers were imbued with the authoritarian ideology of elites. I therefore described the mechanisms by which Brazilian state elites indoctrinated workers in the thirties as well as those by which subsequent elites kept the state ideology alive. I showed that, by erecting the corporative state structures under Vargas's autocratic rule and by preserving those structures to this day, Brazilian elites have used a number of mechanisms of power, which have allowed them to instill and maintain the authoritarian values of the state ideology among urban workers for almost half a century.

If this is the case, what general conclusions can be drawn from this study? Where the theory of the state is concerned, the lesson is unmistakable. Neither orthodox Marxism or neo-Marxism, on the one hand, nor pluralist conceptions of the state, on the other, can help us explain the pattern of working-class formation in Brazil. These approaches favor society-centered explanations of patterns of working-class formation and of class conflict, that is, explanations that rely mostly on social and economic characteristics of the process of capitalist industrialization. These society-centered explanations thus implicitly assume that state actors, state structures, and state policies have a relatively minor role in structuring relations within civil society.

This book is at odds with such society-centered explanations. It shows that state actors and state structures had a fundamental role in shaping working-class action and consciousness as well as in structuring class relations in Brazil.

Without denying the importance of social and economic factors, the analysis presented in this book strongly indicates that the state can play a dominant role in shaping capitalist society. In Brazil, at least, state actors and the state structures they built were capable of securing the consent of the working class, thus obtaining its cooperation in shouldering most of the enormous burden of delayed capitalist industrialization. As this book has shown, Brazilian state elites were remarkably effective in counteracting the exacerbating effect of capitalist industrialization and democracy on class conflict by erecting state structures that shaped working-class action and consciousness in a way that minimized class conflict. This book therefore joins other studies of state elites, state structures, and state policies in offering evidence for a view of the state as an autonomous actor capable of structuring its own relations with society as well as important relations within civil society itself.

However, the purpose of this book was hardly to offer another clear instance of autonomous state action. Its main purpose was to go beyond that, to show *how* the state can secure working-class consent and to reveal the specific mechanisms of power underlying the impact of state actors and state structures on the consciousness of workers. Hoping it would help me understand in greater depth how those actors and structures shape consciousness, I turned to the theoretical and empirical literature centered on the concept of power. Such a move proved gratifying. Looking at the relation between state actors and workers as a power relation, and at state actions and structures as embodying mechanisms of power, was certainly illuminating for understanding the role of the state. But there were other payoffs, as well. The attempt to translate state actions and structures into mechanisms of power also refined existing knowledge about such mechanisms. It was rewarding to discover that the literature on power and that on the state had much, so to speak, to say to each other.

Out of my search for the mechanisms of power underlying corporative state structures I reached the following conclusions. The state elites of the thirties could shape the political consciousness of workers because they facilitated the latter's adaptation to extreme forms of powerlessness. By erecting corporative institutions, they offered both material and symbolic rewards to workers, when they clearly had the power to do otherwise. In doing so, they unambiguously showed workers that they chose benevolence over coercion, thus meeting the powerless workers' strong psychological need to believe in the benevolence of the powerful. These authoritarian elites shrewdly took advantage of the fact that workers had been badly mistreated by previous elites to convince them of the benevolence and superiority of authoritarian elites and regimes. They induced workers to identify with them and gradually to internalize the view of the authoritarian state as their benefactor—a view central to the authoritarian-corporative state ideology. In the end, this meant that Brazilian workers were trapped in institutions that worked against their best interest.

The corporative state structures not only helped diffuse the state ideology, they also kept it alive among workers by means of two powerful mechanisms. In the first place, they effectively preempted the organization of workers by counterelites and prevented the latter from reaching workers in other ways. By insulating workers from counterelites, corporative arrangements prevented them from being exposed to alternative ideas, beliefs, and values. But this is not all. As we saw, corporative institutions also discouraged autonomous political participation. Since such participation is one of the few means by which the disadvantaged can gradually develop a critical consciousness of their social and political environment, corporative structures also prevented workers from developing alternative beliefs and values on their own.

These conclusions are just a beginning, of course. I have merely identified some of the mechanisms of power underlying the operation of only one particular type of state structure. I do hope, however, that I have at least demonstrated the value of engaging in the exercise of identifying the mechanisms of power through which state actors and state structures can manipulate the consciousness and consent of citizens.

APPENDIX

NOTES

BIBLIOGRAPHY

INDEX

Appendix

THE EVIDENCE

THE SAMPLE

THIS BOOK is based on part of a political survey jointly conducted by the Center for Political Studies of the Institute for Social Research of the University of Michigan and the Instituto Universitário de Pesquisas do Rio de Janeiro of the Cândido Mendes University, under the sponsorship of the Ford Foundation. In 1972 and 1973, interviews were conducted with individuals in a sample of 1,314 persons living in six Brazilian states.

This sample was a multistaged area probability sample of the adult (eighteen years and older) population of southeast Brazil. Respondents were selected through a procedure involving five stages. The first stage consisted of selecting six states to represent the southeastern region of Brazil. The selected states were Rio de Janeiro, Espírito Santo, Minas Gerais, São Paulo, Rio Grande do Sul, and Guanabara (largely, the city of Rio de Janeiro), each of which received representation according to its population. Since the combined population of these six states totals 92 percent of the population of the southeast, our sample is very nearly a probability sample of southeast Brazil.

The next stage consisted of selecting *municípios,* a countylike administrative unit of local government comprising an urban-based government with jurisdiction over the surrounding rural area. After being stratified by degree of urbanization, the *municípios* were selected with probabilities proportional to their size (except for capital cities, which were always included). The third stage involved selecting census sectors within the selected *municípios* and dividing them into segments containing a manageable number of dwellings. Next, households were systematically selected from segment listings, and, finally, from within each selected household one respondent was chosen (with known probability).

From a total of 1,527 scheduled addresses, 1,314 interviews were made. Although satisfactory, this response rate of 86 percent yielded a sample that was obviously not free from some distortion. Nonresponse was more frequent within certain groups of the population, which affected the distribution of demographic variables such as sex, age, and urban-rural residence. The unweighted sample estimates of those characteristics were off aggregate population values by a factor of 7 percent in the case of place of residence, 6 percent in the case of sex, and 2 percent in that of age. Therefore, a weighting procedure was used to compensate for nonresponse.

The part of the sample used in this volume included all nonsupervisory wage manual workers in nonagricultural occupations who lived in urban areas (N = 617; weighted, N = 562). Both skilled and unskilled workers in the secondary and tertiary sectors of the Brazilian economy were included. The occupational scale is composed of eight categories: (1) professionals and higher managerial and administrative occupations, (2) lower managerial and administrative occupations, (3) higher nonmanual supervisory occupations, (4) lower nonmanual supervisory occupations, (5) nonmanual routine occupations, (6) foremen, (7) manual skilled occupations, and (8) laborers and semiskilled occupations. Categories 7 and 8 are what I have called *workers* in this book. For a complete listing of occupations as well as for details on the construction of the occupational scale, see Cohen, et al., pp. 276–89.

THE VALIDITY OF THE EVIDENCE

Since interviews were conducted under a repressive military regime, it is only natural to suspect that respondents were afraid of expressing their true opinions. But there are several reasons to believe that, perhaps with only a few exceptions, our respondent's answers expressed their true opinions. For one, I myself directed the fieldwork and interviewed many workers, and it was my impression as well as that of the interviewers under my supervision that respondents were far from being fearful to answer the questions we asked them. We had expected respondents to be suspicious of our intentions, given the political content of the questions. Yet, to our surprise, respondents (especially from the lower classes) were glad to answer our questions and did not show fear or suspicion beyond what is normally expected in any survey.

Every interviewer was asked to fill out a short questionnaire after each interview, which included a few questions concerning the respondent's fear to speak his mind on political issues. According to our interviewers, only a very small proportion of respondents—5–10 percent, depending on the question—showed fear during the interview or had any objections concerning the confidentiality of their answers. Many interviewers expressed great surprise both by the ease with which the respondents answered questions and by their thoughts concerning political matters.

It should also be remembered that some of the questions I used in the present volume were not that threatening to workers. It is hard to see why workers should be so afraid to disagree with the statement that the country would end up in a mess if government paid too much attention to the people, or even to say that the government should not control the *sindicatos* as much as it does. Moreover, workers always had the choice to be neutral in answering threatening questions. Instead of saying, as the great majority did, that they were extremely satisifed with the government, they could have said they were more or less satisfied or neither satisfied nor dissatisfied. Instead of saying, as most did, that they fully trusted the military and the government, they could have said they trusted it more or less, or only sometimes.

There are still other reasons to believe workers were offering sincere answers to our questions. Authoritarian regimes like that of Brazil are highly selective in their repression. Since they also censor the media, repression is largely invisible to a good proportion of the population, especially to those who do not pay much attention to politics in the first place. If this is the case, many respondents would not be sufficiently politicized to even know how repressive the regime was. There are some indications that workers were not fully aware of how repressive the regime was. Almost 90 percent of them did not know of the institutional acts, which were the central pieces of the repressive legislation enacted by the military. One of the acts—the Fifth—has become almost a symbol of the repressive character of the military regime. And there are other indicators of the lack of awareness of workers: 70 percent did not know which party was in opposition, 80 percent said they took no interest in politics, and 84 percent said politics was too complicated for them to follow. It is conceivable, therefore, that many workers did not see much threat in answering questions in less than flattering ways to the military and the military government.

It should be added that respondents were consistent in their answers to a large variety of questions, which were not all politically loaded. It is hard to imagine that they could have dissimulated their true opinions in such a consistent fashion. Their answers were not only consistent among themselves but also consistent with all the evidence we have from other studies of Brazilian workers conducted under the democratic period not long before the onset of the military regime (see chapter 4). The answers workers gave to our questions are therefore far from surprising; they are what we would have expected them to be, given our knowledge of Brazilian history and Brazilian workers.

For the questionnaire given to interviewers as well as for the complete questionnaire applied to respondents, see Cohen et al., appendix.

Notes

CHAPTER 1. INTRODUCTION

1. For accounts of the Brazilian military coup of 1964, see Stepan, *Military in Politics*, esp. parts 2 and 3; Stepan, "Political Leadership and Regime Breakdown"; O'Donnell, *Modernization and Bureaucratic-Authoritarianism*, chap. 2; Skidmore, *Politics in Brazil*, chap. 8; Schneider, *Political System of Brazil*, chap. 2; and Flynn, *Brazil: A Political Analysis*.

2. For what follows, see Skidmore, *Politics in Brazil*, p. 301; and Stepan, "Political Leadership and Regime Breakdown," pp. 123–32.

3. I am here referring to Lipset's well-known argument in *Political Man*, chap. 4.

4. For background on the Revolution of 1930, see Fausto, *A Revolução de 1930*; Carone, *A República Velha*; Skidmore, *Politics in Brazil*, chap. 1; and Flynn, *Brazil: A Political Analysis*, chaps. 3 and 4.

5. For what follows, see chap. 3.

6. For an extensive bibliography on Brazilian corporatism, see chap. 6. For some recent work on the impact of the state on class and class conflict in Brazil and Latin America, see D. Collier and R. Collier, "Inducements versus Constraints"; D. Collier, *New Authoritarianism in Latin America*; Erickson, *Brazilian Corporative State and Working-Class Politics*; Kaufman, "Corporatism, Clientelism, and Partisan Conflict"; Malloy, "Authoritarianism and Corporatism in Latin America"; Mericle, "Corporatist Control of the Working Class"; O'Donnell, "Corporatism and the Question of the State"; Schwartzman, "Back to Weber"; Schmitter, *Interest Conflict and Political Change in Brazil*; Schmitter, "Still the Century of Corporatism?"; Stepan, *State and Society*; A. Souza, "Nature of Corporative Representation"; Wiarda, "Corporatism and Development in the Iberic-Latin World"; and J. Valenzuela, "Chilean Labor Movement."

7. Lamounier, "Formação de um Pensamento Politico Autoritário na Primeira República." A more detailed description of the state ideology is given in chap. 3.

8. For a brief account of this important body of ideas that runs through Aristotle, Roman law, medieval natural law, and Catholic social philosophy, see Stepan, *State and Society*, pp. 26–45. Also see Wiarda, "Corporatism and Development in the Iberic-Latin World."

9. Whereas Keynesian macroeconomic controls are meant as correctives to the functions of the market, the corporatist controls of organic statism are, as Winkler puts it, "antithetical to some of the central institutions of a capitalist economy—the market, profit, and private propery" (Winkler, "Corporatism," p. 111). The kind of state intervention advocated by organic statism goes far beyond Keynesian management. It involves controlling all the major factors usually manipulated by private entrepreneurs to increase their profit; that is, it involves microeconomic controls at the level of the firm. Prices, costs, type, and volume of products, are largely controlled by the state. Organic statism therefore maintains private property but greatly curtails the autonomy of economic actors so necessary for a market to operate.

10. Although organic statism and fascism share some traits, they are fundamentally different in that in organic statism the component parts of society have an important role of their own within the organic whole and are therefore allowed a far greater degree of autonomy than in fascism. This is the "principle of subsidiarity" of organic statism, according to which the subsidiary role of subordinate bodies of society should not be absorbed by the state. For this principle, see Stepan, *State and Society*, pp. 35, 48–52.

11. That illiberal ideologies were functional to delayed industrialization in no way implies they were caused by it. Their emergence may be due to factors that had nothing to do with delayed industrialization. Just because some phenomenon is functional, or beneficial, to some other entity does not mean that the latter is its cause. The sun may help tomatoes grow, but that does not mean that tomatoes cause the sun's existence. In the same way, just because illiberal ideologies are functional to delayed industrialization does in no way mean that late industrialization causes illiberal ideologies. To show otherwise, one would have to identify the mechanism by which late industrialization causes the emergence of illiberal ideologies. If we could specify such mechanism, we would have a functional *explanation* of illiberal ideologies. I have no intention of doing so here, of course. I merely want to suggest that illiberal ideologies are *functional* to late industrialization. I have no intention of explaining their emergence

on the basis of their function to delayed industrialization. For the requirements and problems of functional explanations, see Elster, "Marxism, Functionalism, and Game Theory"; and Elster, *Explaining Technical Change,* pp. 49–68.

12. Gershenkron, *Economic Backwardness in Historical Perspective,* pp. 5–30, 353–66.

13. This is not to say that the state played an insignificant role in the industrialization of early industrializers. The questioning of the myth of the laissez-faire state goes back at least to Polanyi, *Great Transformation.* For a more recent analysis of the role of the early English state, see I. Wallerstein, *Modern World System.* Without denying that the state had an important role in earlier industrialization, one can argue, after Gershenkron, that the greater the backwardness of a country, the greater the role of the state in launching its industrialization. On the role of the state in late-industrializing countries of continental Europe, see Supple, "State and the Industrial Revolution 1700–1914."

14. Gershenkron, *Economic Backwardness in Historical Perspective,* pp. 22–26.

15. The late late industrialization (as Hirschman calls it) of Latin America proceeded in a markedly different way than the late industrialization of the backward countries of continental Europe. As Hirschman has noted, late late industrializers began more gradually, with relatively small plants, and concentrated first on the substitution for imported consumer goods rather than on capital goods. Nevertheless, the latecomers of Latin America had to face a much tougher competition from the advanced countries. There were many more advanced countries to compete with, and the Latin American countries were relatively farther behind them. Even though import-substitution industrialization did not initially require the special institutional devices needed by the late industrializers of continental Europe, the tougher competition under which it had to proceed quickly changed that. Industrialization could be sustained only through a deliberate state policy designed to supply the capital and the infrastructure needed by the nascent industry as well as to protect it from foreign competition. By the early forties, the state in Latin America already had a role in promoting industrial growth, a role highly incompatible with liberal economic doctrine. For a discussion of late late industrialization in Latin America, see Hirschman, "Political Economy of Import-Substituting Industrialization." For general

overviews of the role of the state in Latin American industrialization, see Evans, *Dependent Development;* Furtado, *Economic Development of Latin America;* Cardoso and Faletto, *Dependency and Development in Latin America;* and Veliz, *Centralist Tradition of Latin America.* For the role of the state in initiating Brazilian industrialization, see Baer, Kerstenetsky, and Villela, "Changing Role of the State in the Brazilian Economy"; Dean, *Industrialization of São Paulo, 1880–1945;* Villela and Suzigan, *Politica do Governo e Crescimento da Economia Brasileira, 1889–1945;* and Wirth, *Politics of Brazilian Development.*

16. The construction of the authoritarian-corporative regime is dealt with in chap. 3. Also see n. 6, above.

17. On the relations between the bourgeoisie and the state in Latin America and Brazil, see Cardoso, *Politica e Desenvolvimento em Sociedades Dependentes;* Cardoso, *Empresário Industrial e Desenvolvimento Econômico no Brasil;* Diniz, *Empressário, Estado e Capitalizmo no Brasil;* Diniz and Boschi, *Empresariado Nacional e Estado no Brasil;* Boschi, *Elites Industriais e Democracia;* Leff, *Economic Policy-Making and Development in Brazil;* L. Martins, "Formação do Empresário Industrial"; L. Martins, *Industrialização, Burquesia Nacional e Desenvolvimento;* and L. Martins, *Pouvoir et Dévelopement Économique.* For an insightful analysis of the different types of capitalism and the different state-business relations they entail, see Guimaraes, "Empresariado, Tipos de Capitalismo e Ordem Política."

18. This is well documented in Diniz, *Empresário, Estado e Capitalismo no Brasil,* chap. 3.

19. For a critique of society-centered explanations of working-class formation, see Katznelson, "Working-Class Formation and the State."

20. Ibid., esp. pp. 258–61.

21. Ibid. See also, Katznelson, *City Trenches;* and Shefter, "Trade Unions and Political Machines." For other work on the impact of the state on class, see Brown, "Industrial Capitalism, Conflict, and Working Class Contention in Lancashire, 1842."

22. In the last decade, a considerable number of prominent scholars have argued against mainstream social science for neglecting the state as an actor in its own right. Among them are Berger, *Organizing Interests in Western Europe;* Evans, *Dependent Development;* Evans, Rueschemeyer, and Skocpol, *Bringing the State Back In;* Hamilton, *Limits of State Autonomy;* Katzenstein, *Between Power and Plenty;* Krasner, "Approaches to the State"; Krasner, *Defending the National*

Interest; Nordlinger, *On the Autonomy of the Democratic State;* Schmitter and Lehmbruch, *Trends Toward Corporatist Intermediation;* Skocpol, *States and Social Revolutions;* Skowroneck, *Building a New American State;* Stepan, *State and Society;* C. Tilly, *Formation of National States in Western Europe;* and Trimberger, *Revolution from Above.* See also references in n. 6.

23. For the neo-Marxist debates on the state, see Carnoy, *State and Political Theory;* Gold, Lo, and Wright, "Recent Developments in Marxist Theories of the Capitalist State"; Jessop, *Capitalist State;* and Miliband, *Marxism and Politics.*

24. For this critique of the neo-Marxist literature, see Block, "The Ruling Class Does Not Rule"; Block, "Beyond Relative Autonomy"; Skocpol, *States and Social Revolutions;* and Trimberger, *Revolution from Above.* See also Miliband's critique of Block, Skocpol, and Trimberger in "State Power and Class Interests."

25. For an overview of the literature, see Skocpol, "Bringing the State Back In."

26. Stepan, *State and Society,* p. xii.

27. Ibid.

CHAPTER 2. POWER AND POLITICAL CONSCIOUSNESS

1. Quite aside from the problem that it is often difficult to make inferences from resources to power, conceptualizing power as property also biases one to focus more on the influencer than on the influencee and to overemphasize force to the neglect of more subtle forms of power (power as a zero-sum game). For the problems of seeing power as a property rather than a relation, see Frey, "Concept of Power," pp. 7–10. A useful discussion with interesting examples illustrating the problems of confusing power resources with power itself can be found in Frey, "Distribution of Power in Political Systems."

2. Almost anything can be a power resource: a pleasant smile, the threat to quit a job, and an alluring perfume, as well as tanks, money, and bombs. But under certain circumstances, each one of them can be useless or even a liability. As Baldwin noted, threatening "voters with nuclear attack is not merely one of the less effective ways to win a mayoral election in New Haven; it is a guarantee of defeat." By the same token, possession "of nuclear weapons is not just irrelevant to

securing the election of a U.S. citizen as U.N. Secretary-General; it is a hindrance" ("Power Analysis and World Politics," p. 166). The problem here is that power resources are situation specific, that is, they are not interchangeable. While one can easily convert one economic resource into another through money, there is no such standardized measure of value to facilitate the exchange of political power resources. While the "owner of an economic resource, such as a petroleum field, has little trouble converting it into another economic resource, such as the means to deter atomic attack, he is likely to have difficulty converting this resource into another resource that would, for instance, allow his country to become the leader of the Third World" (ibid.). For other arguments on the fungibility of power resources, see Baldwin, "Money and Power"; and Keohane and Nye, "World Politics and the International Economic System."

3. Frey, "Concept of Power," p. 67. Although I do justify my choice to some extent in the remainder of this chapter, I do not have space for a full justification. Aside from Frey's own defense of his concept, there are a number of reviews of the controversies about the concept of power that can provide further clarification of the concept used in this book. Some of the most useful discussions are Dahl, "Power"; Cartwright, "Influence, Leadership, Control"; Riker, "Some Ambiguities in the Notion of Power"; March, "Power of Power"; Tedeschi and Bonoma, "Power and Influence"; Lukes, *Power: A Radical View;* Nagel, *Descriptive Analysis of Power;* Baldwin, "Power and Social Exchange"; and Wrong, *Power: Its Forms, Bases and Uses.*

4. For a discussion of this issue, see Frey, "Concept of Power," pp. 28–31.

5. For the idea of power as a type of causation, see Simon, *Models of Man;* March, "Introduction to the Theory and Measurement of Influence"; Dahl, "Power"; Nagel, *Descriptive Analysis of Power;* Oppenheim, "Power and Causation"; and Frey, "Concept of Power."

6. Nagel, *Descriptive Analysis of Power,* pp. 9–11.

7. For an extensive discussion of this problem, as well as for suggested solutions, see ibid., chaps. 3 to 5; and Frey, "Concept of Power," pp. 48–63.

8. See Simon, *Models of Man,* chaps. 1 and 3; Simon, "Causation"; and Simon and Rescher, "Cause and Counterfactual." See also Stinchcombe, *Constructing Social Theories,* pp. 34–38; and Nagel, *Descriptive Analysis of Power,* chap. 4.

9. "According to common usage and intuitive understanding, rule by anticipated reaction is a type of power. Indeed, it may be true that power *usually* operates through anticipation of reaction, but the behaviorist definition excludes it from the concept" (Nagel, *Descriptive Analysis of Power*, p. 16). For more details on the "rule of anticipated reactions," a phrase coined by Friedrich, see his *Man and His Government;* Gamson, *Power and Discontent*, p. 69; and Dahl, *Modern Political Analysis.*

10. For Nagel's description of how a definition based on preference incorporates rule by anticipated reactions, see his *Descriptive Analysis of Power*, pp. 28–34.

11. Frey, "Concept of Power," p. 42. Frey's defense is developed in the same paper, pp. 36–47.

12. By autonomous behavior, Frey meant self-directed behavior, of course. Thus, to say that someone behaved autonomously is to say that his behavior was not caused by some other actor. This means that his behavior could not have been the result of an exercise of power. Since no causal link is involved, we cannot speak of a power relation. For a discussion of the notion of "autonomous anticipation," see ibid., p. 43.

13. Ibid.

14. Nagel, *Descriptive Analysis of Power*, p. 18.

15. Frey, "Concept of Power," p. 45.

16. See ibid., pp. 38–39. As Frey pointed out, only a broad definition of behavior can incorporate a number of peculiar power relations. Neither the narrower sense of the term nor any other definition can cope with what Frey has called the "forbearance problem" (p. 46), for instance, or with a situation in which the "influencer does not specifically determine the influencee's behavior, but only restricts or expands his possibilities by altering the perception or appeal of some of his options" (p. 40).

17. This is Frey's definition (ibid., p. 67). See also Frey, "Comment: On Issues and Nonissues in the Study of Power," p. 1081. Because the word *power* has no verb form (to power) and also because it lacks the noun forms for power wielder and power target, Frey uses *influence* as synonymous with *power*. In this way he gains the missing forms: to influence (to exert power), influencer, influencee. I follow this practice in this book. See Frey, "Concept of Power," p. 8.

18. Most students of power believe that power presupposes the existence of conflict. Examples are Dahl, "Concept of Power";

Bierstedt, "Analysis of Social Power"; Kahn, "Introduction"; and Etzioni, *Active Society*.

Even Bachrach and Baratz, vehement critics of Dahl and the so-called pluralists, built conflict into their definition of power. According to them, the pluralists are biased in favor of the status quo because they confine their empirical studies of power to situations of *overt* conflict. By focusing on conflict within decision-making arenas, the pluralists assume that grievances are recognized, articulated, and acted upon and that the political system is open enough to allow any organized group to bring their grievances into decision-making arenas. In so doing, pluralists exclude the possibility that power is exercised to prevent grievances from becoming issues, that is, by keeping potential issues out of politics.

Since for Bachrach and Baratz the suppression of issues is at least as important a means as the more conventional ones of prevailing in decision-making arenas, they argued that the study of power should include the study of "nonissues" and "nondecisions"—that is, the study of how issues that one would expect to arise and decisions that one would expect to be made are prevented from being so. Otherwise, like the pluralists, we would be biased against the downtrodden, whose grievances are kept out of politics. By assuming that the political system is open to any group wishing to press demands, the pluralists assume that the most deprived groups are not prevented from making demands. Rather than being prevented by more powerful groups from participating in politics, their inaction would reflect their own deficiencies. Should they overcome those deficiencies and participate, no one would stop them. Bachrach and Baratz argued that this is not the case; that power is exercised to prevent the deprived groups from participating. But although they stress that *covert* conflict should be included in the study of power along with the *overt* conflict studied by pluralists, they reject the idea that power occurs in the absence of observable conflict.

For critiques of the pluralist conception of power, see Bachrach and Baratz, "Two Faces of Power"; Bachrach and Baratz, "Decisions and Nondecisions"; Crenson, *Un-Politics of Air Pollution;* Frey, "Comment: On Issues and Nonissues in the Study of Power"; Lukes, *Power: A Radical View;* and Gaventa, *Power and Powerlessness*. Bachrach and Baratz's critique owes much to the notion of "mobilization of bias" put forth by Schattschneider, *Semi-Sovereign People*. For attempts to rebut and defend the pluralist method as exemplified by

Dahl's study of New Haven, *Who Governs?*, see Polsby, *Community Power and Political Theory;* and Wolfinger, "Nondecisions and the Study of Local Politics."

19. Frey's definition thus goes beyond Bachrach and Baratz's critique. It implies that power can occur with overt conflict, covert conflict, or with no conflict at all, as is the case when the influencer shapes the very wants of the influencee. Other authors, like Lukes, have argued that the conflict is still there, but in *latent* form, because there is a conflict of interests that is not recognized by the influencee. But, as Frey convincingly argues, power can be exercised even in the absence of a conflict of interests, as in the examples that follow. See Frey, "Comment: On Issues and Nonissues in the Study of Power," p. 1089.

20. This is not the only way in which power is clearly exerted in the absence of conflict (even in the sense of an opposition of interests). There are two other ways: "the influencer's power is the result of the influencee's identification with the influencer, and his concomitant desire to be and to appear to be influenced by him; . . . the influencer has socialized the originally indifferent influencee to want to behave as the influencer wishes him to behave" (ibid.).

21. This is of course an old Marxian argument going back to Marx's conjecture that the ideas of the ruling class are the dominant ideas of a society. For a modern argument on how the bourgeoisie instills false consciousness among subordinate classes, see Miliband, *State in Capitalist Society*. Indoctrination is not the only way to control workers at the level of their consciousness. Keeping them confused is another. For this, see Mann, "Social Cohesion of Liberal Democracy"; and Parkin, *Class Inequality and Political Order,* chap. 3. Although arguments about indoctrination are still more common among Marxists, they are becoming progressively more common among non-Marxists. A recent example of a non-Marxist argument about indoctrination is to be found in Lindblom, "Another State of Mind"; also see Lindblom, *Politics and Markets,* chap. 15.

22. Lindblom, "Another State of Mind," p. 18.

23. Lukes would say that there is a *latent* conflict, rather than *no* conflict, when there is an opposition of interests. Since the expression "conflict of interests" is often used as synonymous with an "opposition of preferences," I prefer to say there is no conflict even when observers spot an opposition of interests that should have been manifested but that is not manifested because power is being exerted.

For the notion of conflict of interests as an opposition of preferences, see Axelrod, *Conflict of Interests*. As for the notion of "latent conflict," see Lukes, *Power: A Radical View*, chap. 4.

24. The classical example of an intention-based definition of power is Weber's, who defined power as the probability that an actor will impose his will on others. See Max Weber, *Theory of Social and Economic Organization*, p. 152. An example is McFarland, *Power and Leadership in Pluralist Systems*, p. 13. For a long list of examples among political scientists, see Frey, "Concept of Power," pp. 22–23.

25. Wrong, *Power: Its Forms, Bases, and Uses*, p. 4.

26. Nagel, *Descriptive Analysis of Power*, p. 20.

27. Frey, "Concept of Power," p. 24. What follows is based on this work, pp. 22–28.

28. See Debnam, *Analysis of Power;* chap. 3.

29. For a critique of this argument, see Frey, "Concept of Power," p. 24.

30. See Wrong, *Power: Its Forms, Bases, and Uses*, p. 4. For a critique of this argument, see Frey, "Concept of Power," pp. 25–26.

31. Frey, "Concept of Power," p. 25.

32. Cited in Erickson, *Brazilian Corporative State and Working-Class Politics*, p. 28.

33. Oliveira Vianna, *Direito do Trabalho e Democracia Social*, p. 26; cited in A. Souza, "Nature of Corporatist Representation," p. 26.

34. Lukes, *Power: A Radical View*, p. 41.

35. Ibid.

36. Frey, "Comment: On Issues and Nonissues in the Study of Power," pp. 1094–99.

37. As Wolfinger noted, strictly controlled comparison is often impossible in the natural world, since too many factors vary simultaneously. But, as Frey noted, this fact cannot be used to argue against the researchability of false consciousness, since it "also is one of the awkward facts facing most social analysis" ("Comment," p. 1096). For Wolfinger's critique, see his "Nondecisions and the Study of Local Politics."

38. In other words, this step is a protective measure against the possibility "that the connections between cause and effect that an analyst perceives in a given situation are not perceived by actors because the connections are not there, or are overridden by connections that actors themselves find more compelling—some significant subset of which might even be justified as 'enlightened choices' "

(Polsby, *Community Power and Political Theory,* p. 230). Or, as Wolfinger would put it, failing to find the expected beliefs might mean either that power was exercised or that the theory leading to our expectations was wrong ("Nondecisions and the Study of Local Politics"). But, again, as Frey correctly noted, this cannot be an argument against the researchability of false consciousness, or other nonissues, because all "cumulative science is tentative for this reason, since additional work is based upon accepted earlier theory which may prove wrong" ("Comment: On Issues and Nonissues in the Study of Power," p. 1096). Furthermore, the analyst is in better shape than Polsby or Wolfinger have suggested, since he can check his theory by identifying what Frey calls the "preventive power mechanism," which prevented the actor in question from holding the expected behavior.

39. For greater details, see appendix.

CHAPTER 3. THE STATE IDEOLOGY

1. I am here referring to the 617 urban workers we interviewed during 1972 and 1973. See appendix.

2. It is possible, of course, that our respondents were afraid of expressing their true opinions and that they therefore disguised their true democratic beliefs. Such a result would be extremely puzzling since, as I shall show, surveys of workers conducted prior to the coup show that they had rather authoritarian political views. If it is true that workers were concealing their beliefs, we would therefore have to conclude that the military democratized working class beliefs, which is, to say the least, rather implausible. In any event, there are other strong reasons to believe that the workers were interviewed in 1972 and 1973 were not lying. For further details, see appendix.

3. For general studies of the Estado Novo, see Skidmore, *Politics in Brazil,* chap. 1; Flynn, *Brazil: A Political Analysis,* chap. 5; Carone, *O Estado Novo (1937–1945)*; and Carone, *A Terceira República (1937–1945)*. For a recent biography of Vargas, see Brandi, *Vargas: Da Vida Para a História.*

4. In 1930 an armed movement deposed President Washington Luiz (1926–30) and the leader of the movement, Getúlio Vargas, became the provisional president of Brazil. This movement, which later became known as the Revolution of 1930, ended the period

known as the Old Republic, which began with the creation of the first republican government in 1889. During the fifteen years of his rule, Vargas ushered Brazil into a new era. He created a modern centralized state and used it to propel Brazil into the industrial era. The literature on the Revolution of 1930 and the period between 1930 and the Estado Novo is extensive. For brief accounts, see Skidmore, *Politics in Brazil,* chap. 1; and Flynn, *Brazil: A Political Analysis,* chaps. 3 and 4. Also see Carone, *Revolucões do Brasil Contemporâneo, 1922–1938;* Fausto, *A Revolução de 1930;* and Levine, *Vargas Regime.*

5. See Skidmore, *Politics in Brazil,* pp. 33–47.

6. Ibid., pp. 43–47.

7. On early industrialization and the impact of the Depression and the war, see Baer, *A Industrialização e o Desenvolvimento Econômico do Brasil,* chaps. 2 and 3; Cardoso and Faletto, *Dependency and Development in Latin America,* chaps. 4 and 5; Dean, *Industrialization of São Paulo, 1880–1945,* chaps. 6–8 and 11; ECLA, "Growth and Decline of Import Substitution in Brazil"; Evans, *Dependent Development,* chap. 2; Furtado, *Formação Econômica do Brasil,* part 5; Hirschman, "Political Economy of Import-Substituting Industrialization"; Luz, *A Luta Pela Industrialização do Brasil;* L. Martins, *Pouvoir et Developement Economique,* chaps. 2 and 5; and Villela and Suzigan, *Política do Governo e Crescimento da Economia Brasileira, 1889–1945.*

8. For the participation of the military, see Skidmore, *Politics in Brazil,* pp. 41–47; Wirth, *Politics of Brazilian Development;* Tronca, "O Exército e a Industrialização Entre as Armas e Volta Redonda (1930–1942)."

9. On the expansion of the federal bureaucracy under Vargas, see M. Souza, *Estado e Partidos Políticos no Brazil,* chap. 4; Daland, *Brazilian Planning;* Graham, *Civil Service Reform in Brazil;* Cunha, *O Sistema Administrativo Brasileiro (1930–1970);* Leff, *Economic Policy-Making and Development in Brazil, 1947–1964;* and Souza Wahrlich, *Reforma Administrativa na Era de Vargas.* On state building in Brazil, see Carvalho, *Elite and State-Building in Imperial Brazil;* Faoro, *Os Donos do Poder;* Schwartzman, *Bases do Autoritarismo Brasileiro;* Schwartzman, "Back to Weber"; and Uricochea, *Patrimonial Foundations of the Brazilian Bureaucratic State.*

10. See Skidmore, *Politics in Brazil,* pp. 41–47.

11. For recent works on the Brazilian corporative system, see Erickson, *Brazilian Corporative State and Working-Class Politics;* and Schmitter, *Interest Conflict and Political Change in Brazil.* For the con-

cept of a corporatist system of interest intermediation, see Schmitter, "Still the Century of Corporatism?"; and Schmitter, "Modes of Interest Intermediation and Models of Social Change in Western Europe." The extensive literature on corporatism and on the Brazilian corporative system is dealt with in greater detail in chap. 6, which is on the workings of corporative institutions in Brazil.

12. Schattschneider was the first scholar to use the expression "mobilization of bias" to refer to the suppression of issues by political institutions. It was subsequently incorporated into the analytical framework developed by Bachrach and Baratz to refer to the mechanisms of power built into political institutions that prevented theatening issues from reaching decision-making arenas. As we shall see, corporative institutions have a variety of such preventive mechanisms. They are probably the most effective institutions for peacefully suppressing issues. See Schattschneider, *Semi-Sovereign People;* Bachrach and Baratz, "Two Faces of Power"; and Bachrach and Baratz, *Power and Poverty.*

13. Lamounier, "Formação de um Pensamento Político Autoritário na Primeira República."

14. What follows is largely based on ibid.; and Santos, "Paradigma e História." Also useful is Oliveira, Velloso, and Gomes, *Estado Novo.* For an excellent study of the political views of the political elite after 1964, see McDonough, *Power and Ideology in Brazil.*

15. Amaral, *O Estado Autoritário e a Realidade Nacional,* pp. 100–01.

16. Campos. *O Estado Nacional,* pp. 61–64.

17. Ibid., p. 61.

18. Amaral argued that the authoritarian state as it existed in Brazil had nothing in common with either the liberal-democratic state or the totalitarian state (both communist and fascist). See his *O Estado Autoritário e a Realidade Nacional,* p. 113.

19. For a discussion of the principle of subsidiarity in organic-statist thought, see Stepan, *State and Society,* pp. 35, 48–49.

20. The differences between doctrinary and instrumental authoritarians are discussed in Santos, "A Práxis Liberal no Brasil," pp. 103–08.

21. Oliveira Vianna is a major Brazilian thinker. For his work see note 22. For the writing of his major followers see Almeida, *Brasil Errado;* Santa Rosa, *A Desordem;* and Santa Rosa, *O Sentido do Tenentismo.*

22. Oliveira Vianna argued that a liberal polity could exist only in a

liberal society. Importing liberal institutions and artificially imposing them on an authoritarian society like Brazil would produce results opposite to those intended, that is, it would only reinforce the authoritarian character of that society. This incongruence between formal political institutions and the true character of society is a main theme of Oliveira Vianna's thought. Oliveira Vianna, *Populações Meridionais do Brasil; O Idealismo da Constituição; O Ocaso do Império;* and *Instituições Políticas Brasileiras.* For his work on corporative institutions, see *Problemas de Direito Corporativo; Problemas de Direito Sindical;* and *Direito do Trabalho e Democracia Social.* For works on Oliveira Vianna see Lima and Cerqueira, "O Modêlo Político de Oliveira Vianna"; and Vieira, *Autoritarismo e Corporativismo no Brasil.*

23. Lamounier describes this state ideology *(ideologia de Estado)* as having eight components: (1) predominance of the principle of the state over the principle of the market; (2) organic-corporative view of society; (3) technocratic objectivism; (4) authoritarian view of social conflict; (5) no organization of civil society; (6) no political mobilization; (7) elitist and voluntarist conception of political change; and (8) the benevolent leviathan. The following pages are a summary of Lamounier's model. See Lamounier, "Formação de um Pensamento Político Autoritário na Primeira República," p. 359.

24. Ibid.

25. Ibid., p. 366.

26. See Vargas's speech to the Constituent Assembly in November 1933, quoted in Erickson, *Brazilian Corporative State and Working Class Politics,* p. 28.

27. See n. 1 and appendix.

28. Erickson, *Brazilian Corporative State and Working-Class Politics,* chap. 6.

29. Souza, "Nature of Corporative Representation," chaps. 7–9.

30. For general accounts of Goulart's government, see Skidmore, *Politics in Brazil,* chaps. 7 and 8; and Flynn, *Brazil: A Political Analysis.*

31. See Stepan, *Military in Politics,* pp. 139–41.

32. For the policies adopted by the military regime and the behavior of the economy after 1964, see Skidmore, "Politics and Economic Policy Making in Authoritarian Brazil, 1937–71"; Fishlow, "Some Reflections on Post-1964 Brazilian Economic Policy"; Bacha, "Issues and Evidence on Recent Brazilian Economic Growth"; Baer, "Brazilian Boom of 1968–72"; Baer, "Brazil: Political Determinants of Development"; Roett, *Brazil in the Seventies;* Ames, *Rhetoric and*

Reality in a Militarized Regime; and D. Collier, *New Authoritarianism in Latin America.* See also n. 12, chap. 4.

33. Weffort, "State and Mass in Brazil," p. 146.

34. Leff, *Economic Policy-Making and Development in Brazil, 1947–64;* M. Souza, *Estado e Partidos Políticos no Brasil (1930 a 1964).*

35. Rodrigues, *Industrialização e Atitudes Operárias,* chap. 4.

36. Ibid., p. 140.

37. See Converse, "Information Flow and the Stability of Partisan Attitudes."

38. For greater detail, see Y. Cohen, "Benevolent Leviathan." Also see McDonough, "Repression and Representation in Brazil."

CHAPTER 4. THE INTERESTS OF WORKERS

1. In *On Liberty,* John Stuart Mill claimed that each person is the *best* judge of his own interest. It is Wolff who has argued that if interest is defined in terms of choice the claim becomes that each person is the *only* judge of his interest. And, since "interest is defined in terms of choice, this is equivalent to the tautology that each man makes his own choice." What Wolff ultimately wants to argue is that according to Mill's subjectivist view whatever an individual chooses to do must be in his interest. On this view of interest, "it is logically impossible for someone to choose against his interests, for his choice is definitive of his interest." See Wolff, *Poverty of Liberalism,* p. 28.

2. Polsby, for instance, clearly admits that he and other pluralists never denied that people could be mistaken about their interests. But pluralists remain subjectivists where their view on interest is concerned in that they admit of mistakes about interests only in the sense that people make factual mistakes about the means they choose to obtain their wants, never in the sense that people can be mistaken about their wants themselves. As Polsby puts it:

> Here are two possible supplementary axioms that state the existence of something like instrumental rationality on a limited scale: (1) The relationships between causes and effects are frequently well and generally understood in a large number of situations in which human beings are faced with choices that have direct consequences for their overall value positions. (2) People generally try to maintain or improve their overall value positions. When people choose not to maintain or improve their overall

> value positions in situations where causes and effects are clearly specified and well known, they can be said to be acting against their interest. This more or less corresponds to an adulterated conception of interests as actors' choices—constrained by an observer's right to override these choices in the event actors do not choose in such a way as to get what they "want." (*Community Power and Political Theory*, pp. 226–27).

3. Barry, "Public Interest," p. 163; and Barry, *Political Argument*, chap. 10.

4. Although these four writers all agree that there are objective criteria by which we can determine what is in the interest of others, regardless of what others think about their own interest, they differ greatly as to the criteria of objectivity themselves. A summary of the points of divergence as well as a critique of Balbus, Connolly, and Lukes is offered by Wall. See Balbus, "Concept of Interest in Pluralist and Marxian Analysis"; Connolly, "On 'Interests' in Politics"; Wall, "Concept of Interest in Politics"; and Lukes, *Power: A Radical View*, chap. 6.

5. Wall has criticized both Balbus and Connolly (Lukes basically follows Connolly) for not recognizing this. He has argued that the defense of objectivism put forth by Balbus is inadequate because the latter said that to have an interest in something is to be affected by it, regardless of whether we know that it affects us or not. In this sense, interest is objective because one can gather evidence to show that someone is unaware of or mistaken about how something affects him. It is precisely this attempt to derive the objectivity of interests from the objectivity of the causal effect something has on an individual that Wall has criticized as inadequate. Wall has rightly criticized Balbus for failing to differentiate the effect something has on someone from the "goodness" (or "badness") of that effect. In other words, a diet may reduce my weight but its objective effect on me does not imply either that it is or it is not in my interest. Similarly, divorcing my wife can affect me in many different ways, all of which can be assessed objectively. But this would in no way allow us to say whether or not divorce was in my interest. To do so would require public criteria to judge the "rightness" of divorcing. Thus Balbus failed to free the objectivist perspective from the necessity of making moral judgments about the choices of others and, therefore, of arguing that such judgments are objective. As for Connolly, Wall argued that his criterion for deter-

mining whether something is in someone's interest is not really an objectivist one—that it ultimately reflects a subjectivist position. Wall argued that this is so because Connolly's criterion does not really allow a judgment of an individual's interest that is independent from his choice. For the quotation, see Wall, "Concept of Interest in Politics," p. 506.

6. I follow here Goodin's definition of manipulation. According to Goodin, manipulation is a form of power in that *A* causes *B*'s behavior without *B* being aware that *A* is exercising power over him. The key feature of manipulation is that the actor who is manipulated is unaware of it. Yet manipulation is not always against the interests of those who are manipulated. As Goodin noted, we "are perfectly comfortable speaking, for example, of manipulating a stubborn old uncle to invest in sound stocks or to go for an annual physical examination" (Goodin, *Manipulatory Politics*, p. 17). This does not mean, however, that people *want* to be manipulated. On the contrary, I would think that, since manipulation can work for or against us, a prudent person would not want to be manipulated. But I am not claiming this. Note that I am not saying that manipulation is against the interests of workers; I am saying that corporative institutions are against their interests because workers do not want to be manipulated.

7. For general accounts of the rise and fall of Goulart's government, see Skidmore, *Politics in Brazil*, chaps. 7 and 8; Flynn, *Brazil: A Political Analysis*, chap. 8; Stepan, "Political Leadership and Regime Breakdown"; Schneider, *Political System of Brazil*, chap. 3; and Dreifuss, *1964: A Conquista do Estado.*

8. For the relations between Goulart and labor, see Harding, "Political History of Organized Labor in Brazil," chap. 10; and Erickson, *Brazilian Corporative State and Working Class Politics*, parts 2 and 3.

9. Erickson showed how radical labor leaders took advantage of the deteriorating economic conditions of the early sixties to call strikes and demonstrations, which they used to pressure Goulart and push their own political program. This does not mean, however, that the more militant labor leaders and the left had a large following among workers. On the contrary, Erickson showed that radical labor leaders had little control over the rank and file and that workers would strike only for narrow economic purposes. These labor leaders appeared much more powerful than they really were, because they skillfully

took advantage of the deteriorating economic conditions and because Goulart allowed them to gain a great deal of organizational control within the corporative structure. Still, the great majority of workers were very suspicious of the radical leaders and would not even take part in the strikes. When asked whether workers should be allowed to strike, 70 percent of our sample said they should not, even if they had good reason to do so. Similarly, Weffort noted that workers were upset with labor leaders because they gave priority to issues of reform and neglected bread-and-butter issues. See Erickson, *Brazilian Corporative State and Working-Class Politics,* pp. 97–150; Weffort, "Sindicators e Política"; and Y. Cohen, "Benevolent Leviathan," pp. 51–52.

10. For accounts of the polarization following Goulart's accession to power, see Santos, "Calculus of Conflict"; and Y. Cohen, "Democracy from Above."

11. For the economic crisis under Goulart's government, see Stepan, *Military in Politics,* pp. 139–41.

12. On the Brazilian economic miracle as well as on its costs, see Baer, "Brazilian Boom of 1968–72"; Baer, "Brazil: Political Determinants of Development"; Bacha, "Issues and Evidence on Recent Brazilian Economic Growth"; Y. Cohen, "Impact of Bureaucratic-Authoritarian Rule on Economic Growth"; Fishlow, "Some Reflections on Post-1964 Brazilian Economic Policy"; Hirschman, "Turn to Authoritarianism in Latin America and the Search for Its Economic Determinants"; Kaufman, "Industrial Change and Authoritarian Rule in Latin America"; Serra, "Three Mistaken Theses Regarding the Connection between Industrialization and Authoritarian Regimes"; Skidmore, "Politics and Economic Policy Making in Authoritarian Brazil, 1937–71"; Skidmore, "Politics of Economic Stabilization in Post War Latin America"; and M. Wallerstein, "Collapse of Democracy in Brazil." Also of interest are Pion-Berlin, "Political Repression and Economic Doctrines"; and Sheahan, "Market-Oriented Economic Policies and Political Repression in Latin America."

13. For the views of the coup makers, see the thorough survey of Brazilian elites by McDonough, *Power and Ideology in Brazil.* See also Hirschman, "Turn to Authoritarianism in Latin America," pp. 76, 80–81; Serra, "Three Mistaken Theses," pp. 110–11, 127–28; Skidmore, *Politics in Brazil,* chap. 8 and epilogue; Flynn, *Brazil: A Political Analysis,* chaps. 9 and 10; Stepan, *Military in Politics,* parts 3 and 4; and Schneider, *Political System of Brazil,* chaps. 4–7.

14. The institutional acts are in the Coleção das Leis do Brasil (Rio de Janeiro: Departamento de Imprensa Nacional). In addition, see Alves, *Estado e Oposição no Brasil (1964–1984).*

15. For data on the purges, see M. Figueiredo, "A Política de Coação no Brasil Pós-64."

16. Erickson, *Brazilian Corporative State and Working-Class Politics,* pp. 153–54.

17. See Schneider, *Political System of Brazil,* p. 189; and M. Figueiredo, "A Política de Coação no Brasil Pós-64," p. 155.

18. Erickson, *Brazilian Corporative State and Working-Class Politics,* pp. 154–55.

19. On the relations between the executive and the Congress, see Abranches, "O Processo Legislativo e Conflito e Conciliação na Política Brasileira"; Abranches and Soares, "As Funções do Legislativo"; Mendes, *O Legislativo e a Tecnocracia;* and Santos, "Calculus of Conflict."

20. See Erickson, *Brazilian Corporative State and Working-Class Politics,* p. 156.

21. Most notable is Schmitter, " 'Portugalization' of Brazil?"

22. On intervention in *sindicatos,* see Erickson, *Brazilian Corporative State and Working-Class Politics,* pp. 34–46, 157–58; Mericle, "Corporatist Control of the Working Class"; and Figueiredo, "Política Governamental e Funções Sindicais."

23. Figueiredo, "Política Governamental e Funções Sindicais," pp. 40–76.

24. For the changes in the social security system, see Erickson, *Brazilian Corporative State and Working-Class Politics,* pp. 159–60.

25. Ibid., part 2.

26. See Mericle, "Corporatist Control of the Working Class," pp. 321–31; and Erickson, *Brazilian Corporative State and Working-Class Politics,* pp. 158–59.

27. Erickson, *The Brazilian Corporative State and Working-Class Politics,* p. 159.

28. Ibid.

29. What follows is based on ibid., pp. 160–67.

30. Between 1967 and 1975, the National Monetary Council's projections were on average almost 10 percent per year below actual inflation. Ibid., p. 163.

31. Ibid., p. 164.

32. Table 5 has been questioned by the Departamento Intersindi-

cal de Estatística e Estudos Sócio-Econômicos (DIEESE), which has published data showing that the real minimum wage did not decline under Goulart. If this is true, workers were even less aware of their interests than I suggest they were. They would have even less reason to be against the Goulart government than they would had their wages in fact decreased under that government. For the DIEESE data, see M. Wallerstein, "Collapse of Democracy in Brazil," pp. 17–20.

33. See Serra, "Three Mistaken Theses," p. 110.

CHAPTER 5. MECHANISMS OF POWER

1. As I have already noted in chap. 2 (see note 18), the exercise of power does not presuppose conflict. As a matter of fact, power can occur in the absence of conflict precisely because its exercise can suppress overt as well as covert conflict. For a more detailed discussion of the mechanisms of power by which conflict is suppressed, see Bachrach and Baratz, *Power and Poverty,* pp. 43–46; and Gaventa, *Power and Powerlessness,* pp. 13–20.

2. Bachrach and Baratz, *Power and Poverty,* p. 43.

3. Ibid., p. 45.

4. Ibid., p. 45.

5. Ibid., p. 46.

6. For a discussion of this mechanism and some examples, see Gaventa, *Power and Powerlessness,* pp. 16–17.

7. For an excellent discussion of these concepts as well as for a critique of mainstream political science studies of socialization, see Lindblom, "Another State of Mind." Also see discussion in chap. 2 of this book.

8. Lindblom, "Another State of Mind," p. 18.

9. For general discussions of this point as well as for evidence, see Moore, *Injustice: The Social Bases of Obedience and Revolt,* chap. 2; Wrong, *Power: Its Forms, Bases and Uses,* chap. 5; Gaventa, *Power and Powerlessness,* chap. 1; and Lukes, *Power: A Radical View,* esp. chap. 8.

10. My discussion of the Untouchables is a condensed version of Moore's, in *Injustice: The Social Bases of Obedience and Revolt,* pp. 55–64.

11. There is a great deal of evidence showing that to a large extent dominant and subordinate social groups share the same political beliefs and values in Western democracies. For some of that evidence,

see Greenstein, *Children and Politics;* Hess and Torney, *Development of Political Attitudes in Children;* Easton and Dennis, *Children in the Political System;* Langton, *Political Socialization;* and Weissberg, *Political Learning, Political Choice, and Democratic Citizenship.* Most of this literature tends to stress the benign aspects of "socialization" or "political learning". Such learning is seen as largely beneficial to the individual and society; it is a "function" that must be performed by the political system. For an exception that looks at socialization as a process of *indoctrination,* whereby the underprivileged are taught ideas in order to accept both their station in life and the status quo, see Litt, "Civic Education, Community Norms, and Political Indoctrination."

12. The critique of capitalist democracies as having an upper-class bias that has no justification in democratic theory is very old. In its most recent form, it criticizes what has become known as a pluralist view of American democracy, as formulated most notably by Dahl *(Preface to Democratic Theory; Pluralist Democracy in the United States;* and *Who Governs?).* For a collection of essays criticizing the pluralists, as well as an excellent bibliography on pluralism and its critics, see Connolly, *Bias of Pluralism.* See also Gamson, "Stable Unrepresentation in American Society"; and Gamson, *Strategy of Social Protest.* Perhaps the most precise articulation of the argument that Western democracies are biased in favor of their corporate elites and the upper classes is Lindblom, *Politics and Markets,* part 5.

13. For some empirical studies of the perpetuation of class inequalities, see Blau and Duncan, *American Occupational Structure;* Jencks, *Inequality;* Bowler and Gintis, *Schooling in Capitalist America;* and Featherman and Hauser, *Opportunity and Change.* For the beliefs of the underprivileged on the fairness of the economic system, see Kluegel and Smith, *Beliefs About Inequality.*

14. R. Lane, "Fear of Equality."

15. Kluegel and Smith, *Beliefs About Inequality,* pp. 72, 124.

16. Ibid., p. 141.

17. Ibid., pp. 72–73, 100–02, 141–42.

18. See Coughlin, *Ideology, Public Opinion, and Welfare Policy;* Lopreato and Hazerligg, *Class, Conflict, and Mobility;* and Mann, *Consciousness and Action among the Western Working Class.*

19. Much of the considerable evidence on this is in Weissberg, *Political Learning, Political Choice, and Democratic Citizenship,* and in the other books mentioned in note 11.

20. For some evidence, see Weissberg, *Political Learning, Political*

Choice, and Democratic Citizenship; Lindblom, *Politics and Markets,* chaps. 15 and 17; and Miliband, *State in Capitalist Society,* chaps. 7 and 8.

21. See Lindblom, *Politics and Markets,* pp. 206 and 227.

22. For this argument, see ibid., pp. 172–87.

23. See Kohn, *Class and Conformity;* and Mueller, *Politics of Communication,* chap. 2, for an extensive discussion of the literature on the subject.

24. On language codes and class, see Bernstein, "Social Class, Linguistic Codes, and Grammatical Elements"; Bernstein, "Language and Social Class"; Bernstein, "Elaborated and Restricted Code"; and Bernstein, "Sociolinguistic Approach to Socialization with Some Reference to Educability." On how political elites control language and communication in order to legitimate the political order, see Edelman, *Politics as Symbolic Action;* Edelman, *Symbolic Uses of Politics;* and Mueller, *Politics of Communication.*

25. See Machado, "Political Socialization in Authoritarian Systems"; Gouveia, "Education and Development"; and Havighurst and Moreira, *Society and Education in Brazil.*

26. Wrong, *Power: Its Forms, Bases and Uses,* p. 112. Wrong's essay on coercion and legitimacy is most useful in pointing out that coercion may be at the root of what are thought of as legitimate political orders.

27. Ibid.

28. Freud, *Ego and the Mechanisms of Defense.*

29. Ibid.,p. 121.

30. What follows is based on Bettelheim, "Individual and Mass Behavior in Extreme Situations"; Bettelheim, *Informed Heart,* chaps. 4 and 5; E. Cohen, *Human Behavior in the Concentration Camp;* Kogon, *Theory and Practice of Hell;* and Bluhm, "How Did They Survive?"

31. Elkins, *Slavery: A Problem in American Institutional and Intellectual Life,* p. 104. Elkins's argument has generated a great deal of criticism. However, he has been mostly criticized for exaggerating the passivity of slaves or for underemphasizing the extent to which slaves rebelled against their masters. But such criticism does not invalidate the argument that the mechanisms of identification and internalization do work. Nor does it invalidate the argument that many slaves, although perhaps less than Elkins suggests, did in fact internalize the values of their masters. For Elkins's critics and his rebuttal, see Genovese, "Rebelliousness and Docility in the Negro Slave"; Frederickson and Lasch, "Resistance to Slavery"; A. Lane, *Debate over Slavery;* and Elkins, "Two Arguments on Slavery."

32. Actually, the process began with the shock of sudden arrest, transportation, and "initiation," which brutally severed the slave and inmate from their past. Faced with an entirely new life, their old values could no longer provide them guides for conduct. These initial shocks, therefore, led them to shed their old values and opened them to new ones. Through their dependence and infantilization, they then internalized the new values provided by their captors. For a description of the entire process as well as for the grim parallel between the transformation of the concentration camp inmate and that of the slave, see Elkins, *Slavery,* part 3.

33. "Here it should be added that the prisoners were also debased by techniques which went much further into childhood situations. They were forced to soil themselves. In the camp defecation was strictly regulated; it was one of the most important daily events, discussed in great detail. During the day, prisoners who wanted to defecate had to obtain the permission of a guard." Bettelheim, *Surviving and Other Essays,* p. 76. These and other techniques ultimately led to a variety of infantile behaviors on the part of inmates. See ibid., pp. 75–83.

34. E. Cohen admitted that "for all of us the SS was a father image." (*Human Behavior in the Concentration Camp,* p. 179); and "Only very few of the prisoners escaped a more or less intensive identification with the SS" (ibid., p. 177). Bettelheim said, "A prisoner had reached the final stage of adjustment to the camp situation when he had changed his personality so as to accept as his own the values of the Gestapo" (*Surviving and Other Essays,* p. 77). See also Cohen, pp. 189–93, on antisemitism among the Jews. It should be noted that the interpretation of these authors has been criticized for the same reasons Elkins's interpretation has been criticized.

35. For the effects of continual defeat, see Gaventa, *Power and Powerlessness,* pp. 16–17.

36. See Katznelson, *Black Men, White Cities,* p. 198; and Korpi, "Conflict, Power, and Relative Deprivation," p. 1571.

37. Moore, *Injustice: The Social Bases of Obedience and Revolt,* p. 23, n. 15.

38. See Lindblom, *Politics and Markets,* part 5; and Miliband, *State in Capitalist Society,* chaps. 7 and 8.

39. For the effect of electoral competition on leftist parties, see Przeworski and Sprague, *Paper Stones.* See also Miliband, *State in Capitalist Society,* pp. 184–98.

40. Garson, "Automobile Workers and the American Dream," p.

163. For discussions of the split consciousness of the subordinate classes, see also Gramsci, *Modern Prince and Other Writings,* pp. 66–67; Mann, "Social Cohesion of Liberal Democracy"; and Gaventa, *Power and Powerlessness,* p. 20.

41. See Pateman, *Participation and Democratic Theory;* and Pizzorno, "Introduction to the Theory of Political Participation."

42. Most of the literature on participation argues that participation is a consequence of a high level of political awareness, which in turn is associated with high socioeconomic status. For this argument, as well as for much evidence supporting it, see Verba and Nie, *Participation in America.* On the other hand, Seeman has argued that participation itself also increases consciousness. See Seeman, "On the Meaning of Alienation"; Seeman, "Alienation and Social Learning in a Reformatory"; Seeman and Evans, "Alienation and Learning in a Hospital Setting"; Neal and Seeman, "Organization and Powerlessness"; and Seeman, "Alienation, Membership, and Political Knowledge.

43. See Verba and Nie, *Participation in America,* part 2.

CHAPTER 6. MAINTAINING THE STATE IDEOLOGY

1. For the evolution of social and labor legislation in Brazil, see Rocha Barros, *Origens e Evolução da Legislação Trabalhista;* Moraes Filho, *O Problema do Sindicato Único no Brasil,* pp. 182–308; Harding, "Political History of Organized Labor in Brazil"; Malloy, "Social Security Policy and the Working Class in Twentieth-Century Brazil"; Souza Martins, *O Estado e a Burocratização do Sindicato no Brasil,* pp. 13–88, 115–35; Rodrigues, *Sindicato e Desenvolvimento no Brasil,* pp. 46–79; Rodrigues, *Conflito Industrial e Sindicalismo no Brasil,* pp. 157–75; Rowland, "Classe Operária e Estado de Compromisso"; Simão, *Sindicato e Estado,* esp. pp. 84–92, 204–05; and Vianna, *Liberalismo e Sindicato no Brasil.*

2. As a signatory of the Treaty of Versailles, the Brazilian government was committed to the International Labor Charter, which required Brazil to provide minimum legal protection for workers. This commitment was reinforced by Brazil's participation in the labor conference in Washington, D.C., in 1919. See Harding, "Political History of Organized Labor in Brazil," p. 47.

3. The strike of 1917 broke out in São Paulo and paralyzed the city as well as most of the state. The strikers extracted important conces-

sions from their employers, including a 20 percent wage increase. Subsequently, however, part of the concessions were withdrawn, and the union leadership was arrested. Nevertheless, the strike gave greater salience to the issue of labor protection and alerted authorities to the potential consequences of neglecting the issue.

4. Before 1930, social legislation was restricted to very few laws protecting women and minors, some provisions on sanitary conditions, a couple of laws extending retirement benefits to a few categories of workers, and (only in 1925) a law giving fifteen days of vacation to workers. See Simão, *Sindicato e Estado*, pp. 84–85, 88–89.

5. In 1911, the State Department of Labor was created as a special organ of the Secretary of Agriculture, Commerce, and Industry (Departamento Estadual do Trabalho). The department had as its central object the working conditions of urban workers, but it had no authority to intervene in labor relations. It did not have the power to supervise the application of labor laws, its function being mainly one of doing research and informing the government on labor relations in the state. In 1923 the National Labor Council (Conselho Nacional do Trabalho) was created, but it was also merely an agency with which the government consulted on matters concerning labor functions. It was only in 1928, when the council was reorganized, that it began to be an organ of enforcement. See Souza Martins, *O Estado e a Burocratização de Sindicato no Brasil*, pp. 20–21.

6. On the labor movement before 1930, see books mentioned in note 1. In addition, see Dias, *História das Lutas Sociais no Brasil;* Dulles, *Anarchists and Communists in Brazil, 1900–1935;* Fausto, *Trabalho Urbano e Conflito Social;* Maram, "Anarchists, Immigrants, and the Brazilian Labor Movement, 1890–1920"; and Pinheiro, *Política e Trabalho no Brasil.*

7. According to Rodrigues, before 1930 labor associations were organized either on a territorial basis or by craft. The transition from craft associations to unions organized by type of industry occurred during the thirties. During the Old Republic, the most important types of workers' organizations were the mutual-aid societies and the resistance leagues; only the first were recognized in law. Whereas the leagues dominated by anarchists and communists rejected the capitalist system and prepared the general strike that was to topple it, the leagues dominated by syndicalists accepted the system and were willing to negotiate, using the strike as their last resort. See Rodrigues, *Conflito Industrial e Sindicalismo no Brasil*, pp. 148–54;

Simão, *Sindicato e Estado*, pp. 149–220; and Erickson, *Brazilian Corporative State and Working Class Politics*, p. 14.

8. On the response of employers to the "social question" and their attitudes toward social legislation, see Dean, *A Industrialização de São Paulo*, part 3; Diniz, *Empresário, Estado e Capitalismo no Brasil*, part 2; Erickson, *Brazilian Corporative State and Working-Class Politics*, pp. 13–14; Fausto, *Trabalho Urbano e Conflito Social*, chap. 7; Castro Gomes, *Burquesia e Trabalho;* Maram, "Anarchists, Immigrants, and the Brazilian Labor Movement, 1890–1920," pp. 19–47; Rodrigues, "Sindicalismo e Classe Operária (1930–1964)"; Simão, *Sindicato e Estado*, chap. 3; and Vianna, *Liberalismo e Sindicato no Brasil*, chap. 2.

9. Quoted in Erickson, *Brazilian Corporative State and Working-Class Politics*, p. 14.

10. See Rodrigues, *Conflito Industrial e Sindicalismo no Brasil*, pp. 154–56.

11. Whereas before 1930 the majority of urban workers were foreigners, between 1930 and 1935 the majority were Brazilian. See Rodrigues," Sindicalismo e Classe Operária (1930–1964)," p. 519.

12. In 1925 a document of the Second Congress of the Communist Party referred to three groups active in the labor movement: the anarchist, the communist, and the "yellow" or "reformist." According to the communists themselves, the latter was dominant. See ibid., p. 531. Also see Fausto, *Trabalho Urbano e Conflito Social*, for reformism in the labor movement prior to 1930.

13. Washington Luiz Pereira de Souza, the last president under the Old Republic, is credited with the statement, "the social question is a matter for the police."

14. Vargas, *A Nova Política do Brasil*.

15. Ibid., p. 73, and also quoted in Harding, "Political History of Organized Labor in Brazil," p. 66.

16. For a chronology of the legislation passed after 1930, see Simão, *Sindicato e Estado*, pp. 85–92, 204–05.

17. See Besouchet, *História da Criação de Ministério do Trabalho*.

18. On the social security system and the labor courts, see Malloy, "Social Security Policy and the Working Class in Twentieth Century Brazil"; and Erickson, *Brazilian Corporative State and Working-Class Politics*, chap. 3.

19. Three unionization laws were passed after 1930, one in 1931, another in 1934 and a final one in 1939, during the Estado Novo. For details, see Souza Martins, *O Estado e a Burocratização de Sindicato no Brasil*, pp. 48–71.

20. The law of 1934 altered that of 1931 in order to adjust it to the liberal Constitution of 1934. The most important change involved the proportion of workers in a given occupational category required to form a union. Whereas the law of 1931 required a proportion of two-thirds, that of 1934 required only one-third. This meant that more than one union could now officially represent a given category of workers. In practice, it was only a partial return to pluralism, since the recognition of more than two unions was virtually impossible. The law of 1939 reestablished the corporative principle of exclusive representation.

21. The unionization law of 1939 was incorporated in the Consolidation of Labor Laws (CLT), promulgated by Vargas in 1943. The CLT is a compilation and systematization of the social legislation passed since 1930.

22. As Humphrey has recently noted, there are at least three different explanations for the continuation of the corporative labor system after the collapse of the Estado Novo. One explanation sees the continuity of the labor system as the result of the incapacity of the Brazilian working class to develop and sustain an autonomous labor system due to the rural background of workers and the uneven nature of industrialization. An opposite view sees it as the failure of the left to take advantage of the situation at the beginning of the democratic period to develop an autonomous labor system. A third explanation sees the continuity as a result of the greater power of the bourgeoisie rather than as an inherent incapacity of workers or their leaders. At this stage, research on the matter is still scarce and insufficient to produce a solid explanation. See Humphrey, *Capitalist Control and Worker's Struggle in the Brazilian Auto Industry*, pp. 18–19. Also see Weffort, "Origens do Sindicalismo Populista no Brasil"; and Vianna, "Estudos Sobre Sindicalismo e Movimento Operário."

23. The description of the mechanisms of control of the corporative labor system that follows is based mainly on Erickson, *Brazilian Corporative State and Working-Class Politics;* Mericle, "Conflict Regulation in the Brazilian Industrial Relations System"; Mericle, "Corporatist Control of the Working Class"; D. Collier and R. Collier, "Inducements versus Constraints"; D. Collier and R. Collier, "Who Does What, To Whom, and How"; Schmitter, *Interest Conflict and Political Change in Brazil;* and Schmitter, "Still the Century of Corporatism?"

24. See Erickson, *Brazilian Corporative State and Working Class Politics*, p. 36.

25. Quoted in Mericle, "Corporatist Control of the Working Class," p. 310.

26. Ibid., p. 315.

27. Erickson, *Brazilian Corporative State and Working Class Politics,* p. 42.

28. Mericle, "Corporatist Control of the Working Class," p. 311.

29. Ibid., pp. 311–13.

30. Schmitter, *Interest Conflict and Political Change in Brazil,* p. 125.

31. These duties are spelled out in Articles 514 and 518 of the CLT. See Erickson, *Brazilian Corporative State and Working-Class Politics,* p. 35.

32. Mericle, "Corporatist Control of the Working Class," pp. 321–22.

33. Ibid., pp. 306–09.

34. See Rodrigues, *Industrialização e Atitudes Operárias,* chap. 3; Lopes, *Sociedade Industrial no Brasil,* pp. 56–69; Erickson, *Brazilian Corporative State and Working-Class Politics,* p. 37; and A. Souza, "Nature of Corporatist Representation," pp. 275–81.

35. A. Souza, "Nature of Corporatist Representation," pp. 413–33.

36. That is why Touraine has called the process by which democracy came to Brazil a "democratisation par voie autoritaire." See "Industrialization et Conscience Ouvrière à São Paulo," p. 87. Similarly, Weffort has noted that the democratic regime of 1946 was radically different from the model of democracy known in Western Europe and the United States, in that "all important organizations that mediate between the state and individuals were, in reality, extensions of the state rather than genuinely autonomous organizations." See Weffort, "State and Mass in Brazil," p. 146. On how the state elite under Vargas perpetuated their power and shaped the democratic regime, see M. Souza, *Estado e Partidos Políticos no Brasil,* chap. 5; and Y. Cohen, "Democracy from Above." For an interesting explanation of the continuity of Brazilian authoritarianism based on Weber's notion of patrimonialism, see Schwartzman, "Back to Weber," pp. 47–78; and Schwartzman, *Bases do Autoritarismo Brasileiro.*

37. For a brief account of the end of the Estado Novo and Vargas's preparations for the democratic period, see Skidmore, *Politics in Brazil,* pp. 39–64.

38. The willingness of opposition elites to cooperate with Vargas

was not only due to strategic considerations. Vargas's capacity to perpetuate his power was greatly helped by the fact the Brazilian elites shared a basic distrust in democracy, a distrust that ultimately favored the perpetuation of a state-dominated society. This is amply documented in M. Souza, *Estado e Partidos Políticos no Brasil,* chap. 3. Also see Almino, *Os Democratas Autoritários.* For the roots of distrust in democracy, see Costa, *Contribuição à História das Idéias no Brasil;* Lamounier, "Formação de um Pensamento Político Autoritário na Primeira República"; Mercadante, *A Consciência Conservadora no Brasil;* Paim, *História das Idéias Filosóficas no Brasil;* and Santos, *Ordem Burquesa e Liberalismo Politico.*

39. On the formation and history of the parties and the party system that emerged during the democratic regime, see M. Souza, *Estado e Partidos Políticos no Brasil;* Soares, *Sociedade e Politica no Brasil;* and Peterson, "Brazilian Political Parties." For a review on the extensive literature on political parties, see Lamounier and Kinzo, "Partidos Políticos, Representação e Comportamento Eleitoral no Brasil, 1946–1978."

40. Campello de Souza has explicitly attributed the weakness and clientelism of the parties and the party system to the fact that they emerged after much power had been concentrated in the state. Since they did not participate in the decision-making process, their function was to purchase support and quiescence through the dispensation of patronage. See her *Estado e Partidos Políticos no Brasil,* pp. 32–33. On the insulation of decision makers in the executive, see Leff, *Economic Policy-Making and Development in Brazil, 1947–1964.*

41. On the Communist Party, see Chilcote, *Brazilian Communist Party;* and Weffort, "Origens do Sindicalismo Populista no Brasil."

42. On Vargas's second government (1941–54), see D'Araujo, *O Segundo Governo Vargas, 1951–1954;* and Skidmore, *Politics in Brazil,* chap. 3.

43. See Rodrigues, "Sindicalismo e Classe Operária (1930–1964)," pp. 533–55; Harding, "Political History of Organized Labor in Brazil," chaps. 6 to 8; Souza Martins, *O Estado e a Burocratização do Sindicato no Brasil,* chap. 2; and Weffort, *O Populismo no Política Brasileira,* pp. 13–97.

44. Erickson, *Brazilian Corporative State and Working-Class Politics,* p. 33.

45. Ibid., chaps. 4 and 5.

46. Erickson, "Corporatism and Labor in Development," p. 151.

47. According to Erickson, radical labor leaders had relatively little control over the rank and file. They appeared more powerful than they really were because they took advantage of special circumstances, such as the deteriorating economic conditions of the early sixties, which were quite independent of their organizational control. They astutely took advantage of these circumstances to call strikes and demonstrations, which they then used for their own political purposes. Goulart finally swung to the left because he believed all along that he could not afford to lose the support of the left and its labor clientele. See Erickson, *Brazilian Corporative State and Working-Class Politics,* pp. 99, 148.

48. Humphrey, *Capitalist Control and Worker's Struggle in the Brazilian Auto Industry,* p. 24.

CHAPTER 7. THE FUTURE OF THE STATE IDEOLOGY

1. On the economic miracle, see n. 2, chap. 4. There is also an extensive debate on the costs of the miracle. On one hand, there are those who defend the policies of the military as beneficial in the long run; on the other, those who criticize the policies as imposing unnecessary sacrifices on the Brazilian population. See Bacha, *Política e Distribuição da Renda;* Bacha, *Os Mitos de Uma Década;* Duarte, "Aspectos de Distribuição da Renda no Brasil em 1970"; Furtado, *Diagnosis of the Brazilian Crisis;* Furtado, *O Brasil Pós-"Milagre";* Hoffman and Duarte, "A Distribuição da Renda no Brasil"; Langoni, *Distribuição da Renda e Desenvolvimento Econômico no Brasil;* Pereira, *Desenvolviemento e Crise no Brasil;* Lurdes Scarfon, *Crescimento e Miséria;* Simonsen and Campos, *A Nova Economia Brasileira;* Simonsen, *Brasil 2001;* Singer, *A Crise do Milagre;* and Tolipan and Tinelli, *A Controvérsia Sobre Distribuição da Renda.* Also important is the controversy over the internalization of the economy. See Bandeira, *Cartéis e Desnacionalização;* Black, *United States Penetration of Brazil;* Evans, *Dependent Development;* Martins, *A Nação e a Corporação Multinacional;* Mirow, *A Ditadura dos Cartéis;* and Hewlett, *Cruel Dilemmas of Development.*

2. On the concentration of power and its effects, see McDonough, *Power and Ideology in Brazil,* Preface and Introduction; and Stepan, "State Power and the Strength of Civil Society in the Southern Cone of Latin America," pp. 331–38.

3. For a useful brief sketch of the evolution of the legitimacy of the military regime, see Souza and Lamounier, "Governo e Sindicatos no Brasil."

4. For the political views of Brazilian elites after the coup, see McDonough, *Power and Ideology in Brazil.*

5. Ibid., p. xxviii.

6. An exhaustive and extensive general survey of the development of opposition to the military regime can be found in Alves, *Estado e Oposição no Brasil (1964–1984).* See also Epstein, "Legitimacy, Institutionalization and Opposition in Exclusionary Bureaucratic-Authoritarian Regimes"; and Stepan, "State Power and the Strength of Civil Society in the Southern Cone of Latin America."

7. On the forms and extent of repression used by the military, see Amnesty International, *Report on Allegations of Tortures in Brazil;* Bertrand Russell Tribunal Session, *On Repression in Brazil, Chile and Latin America;* Biocca, *Estratégia do Terror;* Fon, *Tortura: A História da Repressão Política no Brasil;* Cabral and Lapa, *Os Desaparecidos Políticos;* Klein and Figueiredo, *Legitimidade e Coação no Brasil Pós-64;* and Jordão, *Dossié Herzog—Prisão, Tortura e Morte no Brasil.*

8. On the functioning of the security apparatus and on how its control was a main motivation underlying the process of liberalization, see Stepan, *Os Militares.*

9. See Abreu, *O Outro Lado do Poder;* Góes, *O Brasil do General Geisel;* Kucinski, *Abertura, a História de uma Crise;* and Stumpf and Filho, *A Segunda Guerra.*

10. On the electoral process after 1974, see Lamounier and Cardoso, *Os Partidos e as Eleições no Brasil;* Reis, *Os Partidos e o Regime;* Lamounier, *Voto de Desconfiança;* and Lamounier and Meneguello, *Partidas Políticos e Consolidaçao Democrática.* On the opposition mounted by students, the press, and professional groups after 1974, see Alves, *Estados e Oposição no Brasil (1964–1984),* part 3.

11. For the opposition mounted by the church, see Bruneau, *Church in Brazil,* and Bruneau, "Basic Christian Communities in Latin America."

12. The evolution of the attitudes of the business community toward the military regime is described in Boschi, *Elites Industriais e Democracia;* and Diniz and Boschi, *Emprasariado Nacional e Estado no Brasil.* References on the opposition from the working class are given below.

13. This section on the new, or "authentic," trade unionism is

based on Almeida, "O Sindicalismo no Brasil"; Almeida, "Tendências Recentes da Negociação Coletiva no Brasil"; Erickson, *Brazilian Corporative State and Working-Class Politics;* Humphrey, *Capitalist Control and Worker's Struggle in the Brazilian Auto Industry;* Moises, "Current Issues in the Labor Movement in Brazil"; Souza and Lamounier, "Governo e Sindicatos no Brasil"; Weffort, *Participação e Conflito Industrial;* and Weffort, "Origens do Sindicalism Populista no Brasil."

14. Humphrey, *Capitalist Control and Worker's Struggle in the Brazilian Auto Industry*, pp. 128–29.

15. Ibid., p. 129.

16. Ibid., chap. 4.

17. Ibid., pp. 37–54. Also see chap. 4 of this book.

18. On the new laws concerning job stability, see Ferrante, "História Operária e Legislação Trabalhista"; Barros and Figueiredo, *Creation of Two Social Programs, the FGTS and the PIS;* Cesarino Junior, *Estabilidade e Fundo de Garantia;* and Cesarino Junior, "Encargos Sociais e Fundo de Garantia."

19. See Humphrey, *Capitalist Control and Worker's Struggle in the Brazilian Auto Industry*, chaps. 5–7.

20. On the new strike law see Mericle, "Corporatist Control of the Working Class."

21. Even as late as 1978, the great majority of workers of São Bernardo did not know just who Lula, the popular leader of the metalworkers, was. Humphrey, *Capitalist Control and Worker's Struggle*, p. 158.

22. For this campaign see A. Souza and Lamounier, "Governo e Sindicatos no Brasil," p. 145; Humphrey, *Capitalist Control and Worker's Struggle*, chap. 5.

23. Interview in *Cara a Cara*. Quoted in Humphrey, *Capitalist Control and Worker's Struggle*, p. 155

24. Ibid.

25. Ibid., pp. 166–67.

26. The following is based on ibid., chap. 6 and 7.

27. Alves, *Estado e Oposição no Brasil*, p. 266.

BIBLIOGRAPHY

Abranches, S. H. H. de. "O Processo Legislativo e Conflito e Conciliação na Política Brasileira." Master's thesis, University of Brasília, 1973.

Abranches, S. H. H. de, and Gláucio A. D. Soares. "As Funções do Legislativo." *Revista de Administraçao Pública* (1973): 73–98.

Abreu, Hugo. *O Outro Lado do Poder.* Rio de Janeiro: Nova Fronteira, 1979.

Almeida, Maria Hermínia T. de. "O Sindicalismo no Brasil: Novos Problemas, Velhas Estruturas". *Debate e Critica* (1975): 49–74.

———. "Tendências Recentes da Negociação Coletiva no Brasil." *Dados* 24 (1982): 161–90.

Almeida, Martins de. *Brasil Errado.* Rio de Janeiro: Organização Simões, 1953.

Almino, João. *Os Democratas Autoritários.* São Paulo: Brasiliense, 1980.

Alves, Maria Helena Moreira. *Estado e Oposição no Brasil (1964–1984).* Petrópolis: Vozes, 1984.

Amaral, Azevedo. *O Estado Autoritário e a Realidade Nacional.* Brasília: Editora Universidade de Brasília, 1981.

Ames, Barry. *Rhetoric and Reality in a Militarized Regime: Brazil since 1964.* Beverly Hills: Sage, 1970.

Amnesty International. *A Report on Allegations of Tortures in Brazil.* London: T. B. Russell, 1972.

Axelrod, Robert. *Conflict of Interests.* Chicago: Markham, 1970.

Bacha, Edmar. "Issues and Evidence on Recent Brazilian Economic Growth." *World Development* 5 (1977): 47–68.

———. *Os Mitos de Uma Década.* Rio de Janeiro: Paz e Terra, 1978.

———. *Politica e Distribuição de Renda.* Rio de Janeiro: Paz e Terra, 1978.

Bachrach, Peter, and Morton S. Baratz. "Decisions and Nondecisions: An Analytical Framework." *American Political Science Review* 57 (1963): 641–51.

———. *Power and Poverty: Theory and Practice.* New York: Oxford University Press, 1970.

———. "The Two Faces of Power." *American Political Science Review* 56 (1962): 947–52.

Baer, Werner. "Brazil: Political Determinants of Development." In *Politics, Policies and Economic Development in Latin America*, ed. R. Wesson. Stanford: Hoover Institution Press, 1984.

———. "The Brazilian Boom of 1968–72: An Explanation and Interpretation." *World Development* 1 (1973): 1–15.

———. *A Industrialização e o Desenvolvimento Econômico do Brasil*. Rio de Janeiro: FGV, 1983.

Baer, Werner, I. Kerstenetsky, and A. Villela. "The Changing Role of the State in the Brazilian Economy." *World Development* 1 (1973): 23–34.

Balbus, Isaac D. "The Concept of Interest in Pluralist and Marxian Analysis." *Politics and Society* 1 (1971): 151–77.

Baldwin, David A. "Money and Power." *Journal of Politics* 33 (1971): 578–614.

———. "Power Analysis and World Politics: New Trends versus Old Tendencies." *World Politics* 31 (1979): 161–94.

———. "Power and Social Exchange." *American Political Science Review* 72 (1978): 1129–42.

Bandeira, Moniz. *Cartéis e Desnacionalização: A Experiência Brasileira, 1964–1975*. Rio de Janeiro: Civilização Brasileira, 1975.

Barros, Alexandre de S. C., and Argelina M. C. Figueiredo. *The Creation of Two Social Programs, the FGTS and the PIS*. Rio de Janeiro: Escola Brasileira de Administração Pública, 1975.

Barry, Brian. *Political Argument*. New York: Humanities Press, 1976.

———. "The Public Interest." In *The Bias of Pluralism*, ed. William E. Connolly. New York: Atherton, 1969.

Berger, Suzanne, ed. *Organizing Interests in Western Europe: Pluralism, Corporatism, and the Transformation of Politics*. Cambridge: Cambridge University Press, 1981.

Bernstein, Basil. "Elaborated and Restricted Code: Their Social Origins and Some Consequences." *American Anthropologist* 66 (1964): 55–69.

———. "Language and Social Class." *British Journal of Sociology* 11 (1960): 271–76.

———. "Social Class, Linguistic Codes, and Grammatical Elements." *Language and Speech* 5 (1962): 221–40.

———. "A Sociolinguistic Approach to Socialization with Some Reference to Educability." In *Language and Poverty,* ed. Frederick Williams. Chicago: Markham, 1970.

Bertrand Russell Tribunal Session in Brussels, Belgium. *On Repression in Brazil, Chile and Latin America.* Nottingham: Bertrand Russell Peace Foundation, 1975.

Besouchet, Lídia. *História da Criação do Ministério do Trabalho.* Rio de Janeiro: Serviço de Documentação do MTIC, 1956.

Bettelheim, Bruno. "Individual and Mass Behavior in Extreme Situations." In Bettelheim, *Surviving and Other Essays.* New York: Knopf, 1979.

———. *The Informed Heart.* New York: Free Press, 1960.

———. *Surviving and Other Essays.* New York: Knopf, 1979.

Bierstedt, Robert. "An Analysis of Social Power." *American Sociological Review* 15 (1950): 730–38.

Biocca, Ettore. *Estratégia do Terror: A Face Oculta e Repressiva do Brasil.* Lisbon: Iniciativas Editoriais, 1974.

Black, Jan K. *The United States Penetration of Brazil.* Philadelphia: University of Pennsylvania Press, 1977.

Blau, Peter, and Otis D. Duncan. *The American Occupational Structure.* New York: Wiley, 1967.

Block, Fred. "Beyond Relative Autonomy." In *The Socialist Register 1980,* ed. R. Miliband and J. Savile. London: Merlin Press, 1980.

———. "The Ruling Class Does Not Rule: Notes on the Marxist Theory of the State." *Socialist Revolution* 7 (1977): 6–28.

Bluhm, Hilde O. "How Did They Survive?." *American Journal of Psychotherapy* 2 (1[illegible]8): 2–32.

Boschi, Renato R. *Elites Industriais e Democracia.* Rio de Janeiro: Graal, 1979.

Bowler, Samuel S., and Herbert Gintis. *Schooling in Capitalist America: Educational Reform and the Contradiction of Economic Life.* New York: Basic Books, 1976.

Brandi, Paulo. *Vargas: Da Vida Para a História.* Rio de Janeiro: Zahar, 1983.

Brown, Brian R. "Industrial Capitalism, Conflict, and Working Class Contention in Lancashire, 1842." In *Class Conflict and Collective Action,* ed. Louise A. Tilly and Charles Tilly. Beverly Hills: Sage, 1981.

Bruneau, Thomas C. "Basic Christian Communities in Latin America: Their Nature and Significance." In *Churches and Politics in Latin America,* ed. Daniel H. Levine. Beverly Hills: Sage, 1980.

———. *The Church in Brazil: The Politics of Religion.* Austin: University of Texas Press, 1982.

Cabral, Reinaldo, and Ronaldo Lapa. *Os Desaparecidos Politicos: Prisões, Sequestros, Assassinatos.* Rio de Janeiro: Edições Opção, 1979.

Campos, Francisco. *O Estado Nacional.* Rio de Janeiro: Livraria José Olympio Editora, 1941.

Cardoso, Fernando H. *Empresário Industrial e Desenvolvimento Econômico no Brasil. São Paulo: Difel, 1964.*

———. *Política e Desenvolvimento em Sociedades Dependentes: Ideologias do Empresariado Industrial Argentino e Brasileiro.* Rio de Janeiro: Zahar, 1978.

Cardoso, Fernando H., and Enzo Faletto. *Dependency and Development in Latin America.* Berkeley and Los Angeles: University of California Press, 1979.

Carnoy, Martin. *The State and Political Theory.* Princeton, N.J.: Princeton University Press, 1984.

Carone, Edgar. *O Estado Novo (1937–1945).* Rio de Janeiro: Difel, 1976.

———. *A República Velha.* São Paulo: Difel, 1970.

———. *Revoluções do Brasil Contemporâneo, 1922–1938.* São Paulo: Difel, 1965.

———. *A Terceira República (1937–1945).* Rio de Janeiro: Difel, 1976.

Cartwright, Dorwin. "Influence, Leadership, Control." In *Handbook of Organizations,* ed. James March. Chicago: Rand McNally, 1965.

Carvalho, José Murilo de. *Elite and State-Building in Imperial Brazil.* Ph.D. diss., Stanford University, 1974.

Castro Gomes, Angela Maria de. *Burquesia e Trabalho.* Rio de Janeiro: Campus, 1979.

Cesarino Junior, Antônio F. "Encargos Sociais e Fundo de Garantia." *Conjuntura Econômica* 21 (1967): 57–64.

———. *Estabilidade e Fundo de Garantia.* Rio de Janeiro: Forense, 1968.

Chilcote, Ronald H. *The Brazilian Communist Party: Conflict and Integration 1922–1972.* New York: Oxford University Press, 1974.

Cohen, Elie. *Human Behavior in the Concentration Camp.* New York: Norton, 1953.

Cohen, Youssef. "The Benevolent Leviathan: Political Consciousness among Urban Workers under State Corporatism." *American Political Science Review* 76 (1982): 102–14.

———. "Democracy from Above: The Political Origins of Military Dictatorship in Brazil." *World Politics* 40 (1987): 30–54.

———. "The Impact of Bureaucratic-Authoritarian Rule on Economic Growth." *Comparative Political Studies* 18 (1985): 123–36.

Cohen, Youssef, Philip E. Converse, Amaury G. de Souza, and Peter J. McDonough, *Representation and Development in Brazil, 1972–1973*. Machine-readable data file. Ann Arbor: Inter-University Consortium for Political and Social Research, 1980.

Coleção das Leis do Brasil. Rio de Janeiro: Departamento de Imprensa Nacional.

Collier, David, ed. *The New Authoritarianism in Latin America*. Princeton: Princeton University Press, 1979.

Collier, David, and Ruth B. Collier. "Inducements versus Constraints: Disaggregating Corporatism." *American Political Science Review* 73 (1979): 967–86.

———. "Who Does What, To Whom, and How: Toward a Comparative Analysis of Latin American Corporatism." In *Authoritarianism and Corporatism in Latin America*, ed. James M. Malloy. Pittsburgh: University of Pittsburgh Press, 1977.

Connolly, William E. "On 'Interests' in Politics." *Politics and Society* 2 (1972): 459–77.

Converse, Philip E. "Information Flow and the Stability of Partisan Attitudes." *Public Opinion Quarterly* 26 (1962): 578–99.

Costa, Cruz. *Contribuição à História das Idéias no Brasil*. Rio de Janeiro: Civilização Brasileira, 1967.

Coughlin, R. M. *Ideology, Public Opinion, and Welfare Policy*. Berkeley: Institute of International Studies, 1980.

Crenson, Matthew. *The Un-Politics of Air Pollution: A Study of Nondecisionmaking in the Cities*. Baltimore: John Hopkins University Press, 1971.

Cunha, Mário Wagner Vieira da. *O Sistema Administrativo Brasileiro (1930–1970)*. Rio de Janeiro: Civilização Brasileira, 1971.

Dahl, Robert A. "The Concept of Power." *Behavioral Science* 2 (1957): 201–15.

———. *Modern Political Analysis*. Englewood Cliffs: Prentice-Hall, 1970.

———. *Pluralist Democracy in the United States: Conflict and Consent*. Chicago: Rand McNally, 1967.

———. "Power." *International Encyclopedia of the Social Sciences*. Vol. 12. New York: Free Press, 1968.

———. *A Preface to Democratic Theory*. Chicago: Chicago University Press, 1956.

———. *Who Governs?* New Haven: Yale University Press, 1961.

Daland, Robert T. *Brazilian Planning.* Chapel Hill: University of North Carolina Press, 1967.

D'Araujo, Maria Celina Soares. *O Segundo Governo Vargas, 1951–1954.* Rio de Janeiro: Zahar, 1982.

Dean, Warren. *A Industrialização de São Paulo.* São Paulo: Difel, 1971.

———. *The Industrialization of São Paulo, 1880–1945.* Austin: University of Texas Press, 1969.

Debnam, Geoffrey. *The Analysis of Power: Core Elements and Structure.* New York: St. Martin's, 1984.

Dias, Everado. *História das Lutas Sociais no Brasil.* São Paulo: Edaglit, 1962.

Diniz, Eli. *Empresário, Estado e Capitalismo no Brasil: 1930–1945.* Rio de Janeiro: Paz e Terra, 1978.

Diniz, Eli, and Renato R. Boschi. *Empresariado Nacional e Estado no Brasil.* Rio de Janeiro: Forense-Universitária, 1978.

Dreifuss, René A. *1964: A Conquista do Estado.* Petrópolis: Vozes, 1981.

Duarte, José Carlos. "Aspectos de Distribuição da Renda no Brasil em 1970." Master's thesis, University of São Paulo, 1971.

Dulles, John W. F. *Anarchists and Communists in Brazil, 1900–1935.* Austin: University of Texas Press, 1963.

Easton, David, and Jack Dennis. *Children in the Political System.* New York: McGraw Hill, 1969.

ECLA. "The Growth and Decline of Import Substitution in Brazil." *Economic Bulletin for Latin America* 9 (1965): 1–61.

Edelman, Murray. *Politics as Symbolic Action: Mass Arousal and Quiescence.* Chicago: Markham, 1971.

———. *The Symbolic Uses of Politics.* Urbana: University of Illinois Press, 1967.

Elkins, Stanley M. *Slavery: A Problem in American Institutional and Intellectual Life.* Chicago: University of Chicago Press, 1976.

———. "The Two Arguments on Slavery." In Elkins, *Slavery: A Problem in American Institutional and Intellectual Life.* Chicago: University of Chicago Press, 1976.

Elster, Jon. *Explaining Technical Change.* Cambridge: Cambridge University Press, 1983.

———. "Marxism, Functionalism, and Game Theory." *Theory and Society* 11 (1982): 453–82.

Epstein, Edward C. "Legitimacy, Institutionalization and Opposition in Exclusionary Bureaucratic-Authoritarian Regimes: The Situation of the 1980s." *Comparative Politics* 17 (1984): 37–54.

Erickson, Kenneth P. *The Brazilian Corporative State and Working-Class Politics.* Berkeley and Los Angeles: University of California Press, 1977.

Etzioni, Amitai. *The Active Society.* New York: Free Press, 1968.

Evans, Peter. *Dependent Development: The Alliance of Multinational, State and Local Capital in Brazil.* Princeton: Princeton University Press, 1979.

Evans, Peter, D. Rueschemeyer, and T. Skocpol, eds. *Bringing the State Back In.* Cambridge: Cambridge University Press, 1985.

Faoro, Raymundo. *Os Donos do Poder.* Pôrto Alegre: Editora Globo, 1958.

Fausto, Boris. *A Revolução de 1930: Historiografia e História.* São Paulo: Brasiliense, 1983.

———. *Trabalho Urbano e Conflito Social.* São Paulo: Difel, 1976.

Featherman, D. L., and R. M. Hauser. *Opportunity and Change.* New York: Academic Press, 1978.

Ferrante, Vera Lúcia Botta. "História Operária e Legislação Trabalhista: O. F.G.T.S. e a Perda da Estabilidade." *Escrito Ensaio* 2 (1978): 43–50.

Figueiredo, Argelina M. C. "Política Governamental e Funções Sindicais." Master's thesis, University of São Paulo, 1975.

Figueiredo, Marcus F. "A Política de Coação no Brasil Pós-64." In *Legitimidade e Coação no Brasil Pós-64,* ed. Lúcia Klein and Marcus Figueiredo. Rio de Janeiro: Forense, 1978.

Fishlow, Albert. "Some Reflections on Post-1964 Brazilian Economic Policy." In *Authoritarian Brazil,* ed. Alfred Stepan. New Haven: Yale University Press, 1973.

Flynn, Peter. *Brazil: A Political Analysis.* Boulder: Westview, 1983.

Fon, Antonio C. *Tortura: A História da Repressão Politica no Brasil.* São Paulo: Global, 1979.

Frederickson, M., and C. Lasch. "Resistance to Slavery." *Civil War History* 13 (1967): 315–29.

Freud, Anna. *The Ego and the Mechanisms of Defense.* London: Hogarth, 1948.

Frey, Frederick W. "Comment: On Issues and Nonissues in the Study of Power." *American Political Science Review* 65 (1971): 1081–101.

———. "The Concept of Power." Paper presented at the Annual Meeting of the International Studies Association, St. Louis, 1977.

———. "The Distribution of Power in Political Systems." Paper presented at the annual meeting of the International Political Science Association, Paris, 1985.

Friedrich, Carl J. *Man and His Government.* New York: McGraw Hill, 1963.

Furtado, Celso. *O Brasil Pós-"Milagre."* Rio de Janeiro: Paz e Terra, 1981.

———. *Diagnosis of the Brazilian Crisis.* Berkeley and Los Angeles: University of California Press, 1975.

———. *Economic Development of Latin America: A Survey from Colonial Times to the Cuban Revolution.* Cambridge: Cambridge University Press, 1970.

———. *Formação Econômica do Brasil.* São Paulo: Editora Nacional, 1969.

Gamson, William A. *Power and Discontent.* Homewood, Ill.: Dorsey, 1968.

———. "Stable Unrepresentation in American Society." *American Behavioral Scientist* 12 (1986): 15–21.

———. *The Strategy of Social Protest.* Homewood: Dorsey, 1975.

Garson, David. "Automobile Workers and the American Dream." *Politics and Society* 3 (1973): 163–79.

Gaventa, John. *Power and Powerlessness: Quiescence and Rebellion in an Appalachian Valley.* Urbana: University of Illinois Press, 1980.

Genovese, Eugene D. "Rebelliousness and Docility in the Negro Slave: A Critique of the Elkins Thesis." In Genovese, *In Red and Black.* Knoxville: University of Tennessee Press, 1984.

———. *In Red and Black.* Knoxville: University of Tennessee Press, 1984.

Gershenkron, Alexander. *Economic Backwardness in Historical Perspective.* Cambridge: Harvard University Press, 1966.

Góes, Walder de. *O Brasil do General Geisel: Estudo do Processo de Tomada de Decisão no Regime Militar-Burocrático.* Rio de Janeiro: Nova Fronteira, 1978.

Gold, David A., C. Y. H. Lo, and E. O. Wright. "Recent Developments in Marxist Theories of the Capitalist State." *Monthly Review* 27 (1975): 29–43, 36–51.

Goodin, Robert E. *Manipulatory Politics.* New Haven: Yale University Press, 1980.

Gouveia, Aparecida Joly. "Education and Development: Opinions of Secondary School Teachers." In *Elites in Latin America,* ed.

S. M. Lipset and A. Solari. New York: Oxford University Press, 1967.

Graham, Lawrence S. *Civil Service Reform in Brazil.* Austin: University of Texas Press, 1968.

Gramsci, Antonio. *The Modern Prince and Other Writings.* New York: International Publishers, 1957.

Greenstein, Fred I. *Children and Politics.* New Haven: Yale University Press, 1965.

Guimarães, Cesar. "Empresariado, Tipos de Capitalismo e Ordem Política." In *Estado e Capitalismo no Brasil,* ed. Carlos E. Martins. São Paulo: HUCITEC, 1977.

Hamilton, Nora. *The Limits of State Autonomy: Post-Revolutionary Mexico.* Princeton: Princeton University Press, 1982.

Harding, Timothy F. "The Political History of Organized Labor in Brazil." Ph.D. Diss., Stanford University, 1973.

Havighurst, R. J., and J. Roberto Moreira. *Society and Education in Brazil.* Pittsburgh: University of Pittsburgh Press, 1965.

Hess, Robert D., and Judith V. Torney. *The Development of Political Attidues in Children.* Garden City: Doubleday, 1968.

Hewlett, Sylvia A. *The Cruel Dilemmas of Development: Twentieth Century Brazil.* New York: Basic Books, 1980.

Hirschman, A. O. "The Political Economy of Import-Substituting Industrialization." In Hirschman, *A Bias for Hope.* New Haven: Yale University Press, 1971.

———. "The Turn to Authoritarianism in Latin America and the Search for its Economic Determinants." In *The New Authoritarianism in Latin America,* ed. David Collier. Princeton: Princeton University Press, 1979.

Hoffman, Rodolfo, and João Carlos Duarte. "A Distribuição da Renda no Brasil." *Revista de Administração de Empresas* 14 (1972): 46–66.

Humphrey, John. *Capitalist Control and Worker's Struggle in the Brazilian Auto Industry.* Princeton: Princeton University Press, 1982.

Jencks, Christopher. *Inequality.* New York: Basic Books, 1972.

Jessop, Bob. *The Capitalist State: Marxist Theories and Methods.* New York: New York University Press, 1982.

Jordão, Fernando. *Dossiê Herzog—Prisão, Tortura e Morte no Brasil.* São Paulo: Global, 1979.

Kahn, Robert L. "Introduction." In *Power and Conflict,* ed. R. L. Kahn and E. Boulding. New York: Basic Books, 1964.

Katzenstein, Peter, ed. *Between Power and Plenty: Foreign Economic*

Policies of Advanced Industrial States. Madison: University of Wisconsin Press, 1978.

Katznelson, Ira. *Black Men, White Cities*. New York: Oxford University Press, 1973.

———. *City Trenches: Urban Politics and the Patterning of Class in the United States*. New York: Pantheon, 1981.

———. "Working-Class Formation and the State: Nineteenth-Century England in American Perspective." In *Bringing the State Back In*, ed. Peter B. Evans, D. Rueschemeyer, and Theda Skocpol. Cambridge: Cambridge University Press, 1985.

Kaufman, Robert. "Corporatism, Clientelism, and Partisan Conflict." In *Authoritarianism and Corporatism in Latin America*, ed. James M. Malloy. Pittsburgh: University of Pittsburgh Press, 1977.

———. "Industrial Change and Authoritarian Rule in Latin America." In *The New Authoritarianism in Latin America*, ed. D. Collier. Princeton: Princeton University Press, 1979.

Keohane, Robert O., and Joseph S. Nye, Jr. "World Politics and the International Economic System." In *The Future of the International Economic Order: An Agenda for Research*, ed. C. Fred Bergsten. Lexington: Lexington Books, 1973.

Klein, Lúcia, and Marcus Figueiredo. *Legitimidade e Coação no Brasil Pós-64*. Rio de Janeiro: Forense, 1978.

Kluegel, James R., and E. R. Smith. *Beliefs About Inequality: Americans' Views of What Is and What Ought to Be*. New York: Aldine de Gruyter, 1986.

Kogon, Eugene. *The Theory and Practice of Hell*. New York: Farrar, Strauss, 1946.

Kohn, Melvin L. *Class and Conformity*. Homewood: Dorsey, 1970.

Korpi, Walter. "Conflict, Power, and Relative Deprivation." *American Political Science Review* 68 (1974): 1569–78.

Krasner, Stephen D. "Approaches to the State: Alternative Conceptions and Historical Dynamics." *Comparative Politics* 16 (1984): 223–46.

———. *Defending the National Interest: Raw Materials, Investments, and U.S. Foreign Policy*. Princeton: Princeton University Press, 1978.

Kucinski, Bernardo. *Abertura, a História de uma Crise*. São Paulo: Brasil Debates, 1982.

Lamounier, Bolivar. "Formação de um Pensamento Político Autoritário na Primeira República. Uma Interpretação." In *História*

Geral de Civilização Brasileira. Tomo 3, vol. 2. São Paulo: Difel, 1977.

———. *Voto de Desconfiança: Eleições e Mudança Política no Brasil, 1970–1979.* Rio de Janeiro: Vozes, 1980.

Lamounier, Bolivar, and Fernando H. Cardoso, eds. *Os Partidos e as Eleições no Brasil.* Rio de Janeiro: Paz e Terra, 1975.

Lamounier, Bolivar, and M. D. G. Kinzo. "Partidos Políticos, Representação e Comportamento Eleitoral no Brasil, 1946–1978." *Dados* 19, suplemento, (1978): 11–32.

Lane, Ann J., ed. *The Debate over Slavery: Stanley Elkins and His Critics.* Urbana: University of Illinois Press, 1971.

Lane, Robert E. "The Fear of Equality." *American Political Science Review* 53 (1959): 35–51.

Langoni, Carlos G. *Distribuição da Renda e Desenvolvimento Econômico no Brasil.* Rio de Janeiro: Expressão e Cultura, 1973.

Langton, Kenneth P. *Political Socialization.* New York: Oxford University Press, 1969.

Leff, Nathaniel H. *Economic Policy-Making and Development in Brazil, 1947–1964). New York: Wiley, 1968.*

Levine, R. M. The Vargas Regime: The Critical Years, 1934–1938. New York: Columbia University Press, 1970.

Lima, M. R. S., and E. D. Cerqueira. "O Modêlo Político de Oliveira Vianna." *Revista Brasileira de Estudos Políticos* (1971): 85–109.

Lindblom, Charles E. "Another State of Mind." *American Political Science Review* 76 (1982): 9–21.

———. *Politics and Markets.* New York: Basic Books, 1977.

Lipset, S. M. *Political Man.* New York: Anchor Books, 1963.

Litt, Edgar. "Civic Education, Community Norms, and Political Indoctrination." *American Sociological Review* 28 (1963): 69–74.

Lopes, Juarez R. B. *Sociedade Industrial no Brasil.* São Paulo: Difel, 1964.

Lopreato, J., and L. W. Hazerligg. *Class, Conflict, and Mobility.* San Francisco: Chandler, 1972.

Lukes, Steven. *Power: A Radical View.* London: Macmillan, 1974.

Lurdes Scarfon, Maria de. *Crescimento e Miséria.* São Paulo: Símbolo, 1979.

Luz, Nícia V. *A Luta Pela Industrialização do Brasil: 1808–1930.* São Paulo: Difel, 1960.

McDonough, Peter J. *Power and Ideology in Brazil.* Princeton: Princeton University Press, 1981.

———. "Repression and Representation in Brazil." *Comparative Politics* 14 (1982): 73–99.

McFarland, Andrew S. *Power and Leadership in Pluralist Systems.* Palo Alto: Stanford University Press, 1969.

Machado, Mário B. "Political Socialization in Authoritarian Systems: The Case of Brazil." Ph.D. diss., University of Chicago, 1975.

Malloy, James M. "Authoritarianism and Corporatism in Latin America: The Modal Pattern." In *Authoritarianism and Corporatism in Latin America*, ed. J. M. Malloy. Pittsburgh: University of Pittsburgh Press, 1977.

———. "Social Security Policy and the Working Class in Twentieth-Century Brazil." *Journal of Inter-American Studies and World Affairs* 19 (1977): 35–60.

Mann, Michael. *Consciousness and Action among the Western Working Class.* London: Macmillan, 1973.

———. "The Social Cohesion of Liberal Democracy." *American Sociological Review* 35 (June 1970): 423–39.

Maram, Sheldon. "Anarchists, Immigrants, and the Brazilian Labor Movement, 1890–1920." Ph.D. diss., University of California, Santa Barbara, 1972.

March, James G. "An Introduction to the Theory and Measurement of Influence." *American Political Science Review* 49 (1955): 431–51.

———. "The Power of Power." In *Varieties of Political Theory*, ed. David Eston. Englewood Cliffs: Prentice-Hall, 1966.

Martins, Luciano. "Formação do Empresário Industrial." *Revista Civilizaçao Brasileira* (1967): 91–132.

———. *Industrialização , Burquesia Nacional e Desenvolvimento.* Rio de Janeiro: Saga, 1968.

———. *A Nação e a Corporação Multinacional: A Política das Emprêsas no Brasil e na América Latina.* Rio de Janeiro: Paz e Terra, 1975.

———. *Pouvoir et Dévelopement Economique: Formation et Evolution des Structures Politiques au Brésil.* Paris: Editions Anthropos, 1976.

Mendes, Candido, ed. *O Legislativo e a Tecnocracia.* Rio de Janeiro: Imago Editora, 1975.

Mercadante, Paulo. *A Consciência Conservadora no Brasil.* Rio de Janeiro: Nova Fronteira, 1980.

Mericle, Kenneth S. "Conflict Regulation in the Brazilian Industrial Relations System." Ph.D. diss., University of Wisconsin, 1974.

———. "Corporatist Control of the Working Class: Authoritarian

Brazil since 1964." In *Authoritarianism and Corporatism in Latin America*, ed. J. M. Malloy. Pittsburgh: University of Pittsburgh Press, 1977.

Miliband, Ralph. *Marxism and Politics.* Oxford: Oxford University Press, 1977.

———. "State Power and Class Interests." *New Left Review* (1983): 57–68.

———. *The State in Capitalist Society.* New York: Basic Books, 1969.

Mirow, Kurt. *A Ditadura dos Cartéis: Anatomia de Um Subdesenvolvimento.* Rio de Janeiro: Civilizaçao Brasileira, 1978.

Moisés, José A. "Current Issues in the Labor Movement in Brazil." *Latin American Perspectives* (1979): 51–70.

Moore, Barrington, Jr. *Injustice: The Social Bases of Obedience and Revolt.* New York: Sharpe, 1978.

Moraes Filho, Evaristo de. *O Problema do Sindicato Único no Brasil.* São Paulo: Alfa-Ômega, 1978.

Mueller, Claus. *The Politics of Communication: A Study in the Political Sociology of Language, Socialization, and Legitimation.* New York: Oxford University Press, 1973.

Nagel, Jack H. *The Descriptive Analysis of Power.* New Haven: Yale University Press, 1975.

Neal, Arthur G., and Melvin Seeman. "Organization and Powerlessness: A Test of the Mediation Hypothesis." *American Sociological Review* 29 (1964): 216–26.

Nordlinger, Eric. *On the Autonomy of the Democratic State.* Cambridge: Harvard University Press, 1981.

O'Donnell, Guillermo A. "Corporatism and the Question of the State." In *Authoritarianism and Corporatism in Latin America*, ed. J. M. Malloy. Pittsburgh: University of Pittsburgh Press, 1977.

———. *Modernization and Bureaucratic-Authoritarianism.* Berkeley: Institute of International Studies, 1979.

Oliveira, Lúcia L., M. P. Velloso, and A. M. C. Gomes. *Estado Novo: Ideologia e Poder.* Rio de Janeiro: Zahar, 1982.

Oliveira Vianna, Francisco José de. *Direito do Trabaho e Democracia Social: O Problema da Incorporação do Trabalhador no Estado.* Rio de Janeiro: José Olympio, 1951.

———. *O Idealismo da Constituição.* São Paulo: Companhia Editora Nacional, 1939.

———. *Instituições Politicas Brasileiras.* Rio de Janeiro: José Olympio, 1949.

———. *O Ocaso do Império.* Rio de Janeiro, 1925.

———. *Populações Meridionais do Brasil.* Vol. 1. São Paulo: Companhia Editora Nacional, 1938.

———. *Problemas de Direito Corporativo.* Rio de Janeiro: José Olympio, 1938.

———. *Problemas de Direito Sindical.* Rio de Janeiro: Max Limonad, 1943.

Oppenheim, Felix E. "Power and Causation." In *Power and Political Theory: Some European Perspectives,* ed. Brian Barry. London: Wiley, 1976.

Paim, Antônio. *História das Idéias Filosóficas no Brasil.* São Paulo, 1967.

Parkin, Frank. *Class Inequality and Political Order.* New York: Praeger, 1974.

Pateman, Carole. *Participation and Democratic Theory.* London: Cambridge University Press, 1970.

Pereira, Luiz Carlos Bresser. *Desenvolvimento e Crise no Brasil.* São Paulo: Brasiliense, 1977.

Peterson, Phillys J. "Brazilian Political Parties: Formation, Organization and Leadership." Ph.D. diss., University of Michigan, 1962.

Pinheiro, Paulo Sérgio. *Política e Trabalho no Brasil.* Rio de Janeiro: Paz e Terra, 1975.

Pion-Berlin, David. "Political Repression and Economic Doctrines." *Comparative Political Studies* 16 (1983): 37–66.

Pizzorno, Allesandro. "An Introduction to the Theory of Political Participation." *Social Science Information* 9 (1970): 29–64.

Polanyi, Karl. *The Great Transformation.* Boston: Beacon, 1944.

Polsby, Nelson W. *Community Power and Political Theory.* New Haven: Yale University Press, 1980.

Przeworski, Adam, and John Sprague. *Paper Stones.* Chicago: University of Chicago Press, 1987.

Reis, Fábio Wanderley. *Os Partidos e o Regime.* São Paulo: Símbolo, 1980.

Riker, William. "Some Ambiguities in the Notion of Power." *American Political Science Review* 58 (1964): 341–49.

Rocha Barros, Alberto da. *Origens e Evolução da Legislação Trabalhista.* Rio de Janeiro: Laemmert, 1969.

Rodrigues, José Albertino. *Sindicato e Desenvolvimento no Brasil.* São Paulo: Símbolo, 1979.

Rodrigues, Leôncio Martins. *Conflito Industrial e Sindicalismo no Brasil.* São Paulo: Difusão Européia do Livro, 1966.

———. *Industrialização e Atitudes Operárias.* São Paulo: Brasiliense, 1970.

———. "Sindicalismo e Classe Operária (1930–1964)." In *História Geral da Civilização Brasileira.* Tome 2, vol. 3. São Paulo: Difel, 1981.

Roett, Riordan, ed. *Brazil in the Seventies.* Washington, D.C.: American Enterprise Institute, 1976.

Rowland, Robert. "Classe Operária e Estado de Compromisso: Origens Estruturais da Legislação Trabalhista e Sindical." *Estudos CEBRAP* 8 (1974): 5–40.

Santa Rosa, Virgínio. *A Desordem.* Rio de Janeiro: Schmidt Editor, 1932.

———. *O Sentido do Tenentismo.* São Paulo: Alfa-Ômega, 1976.

Santos, Wanderley Guilherme dos. "The Calculus of Conflict: Impasse in Brazilian Politics and the Crisis of 1964." Ph.D. diss., Stanford University, 1979.

———. *Ordem Burguesa e Liberalismo Político.* São Paulo: Duas Cidades, 1978.

———. "Paradigma e História: A Ordem Burguesa na Imaginação Social Brasileira." In W. G. dos Santos, *Ordem Burguesa e Liberalism o Político.* São Paulo: Duas Cidades, 1978.

———. "A Práxis Liberal no Brasil: Propostas para Reflexão e Pesquisa." In Santos, *Ordem Burguesa e Liberalismo Político.* São Paulo: Duas Cidades, 1978.

Schattschneider, E. E. *The Semi-Sovereign People.* New York: Holt, Rinehart, and Winston, 1960.

Schmitter, Philippe C. *Interest Conflict and Political Change in Brazil.* Stanford: Stanford University Press, 1971.

———. "Modes of Interest Intermediation and Models of Social Change in Western Europe." In *Trends Toward Corporatist Intermediation,* ed. P. C. Schmitter and G. Lehmbruch. Beverly Hills: Sage, 1979.

———. "The 'Portugalization' of Brazil?." In *Authoritarian Brazil,* ed. Alfred Stepan. New Haven: Yale University Press, 1971.

———. "Still the Century of Corporatism?." In *The New Corporatism,* ed. F. B. Pike and T. Stritch. Notre Dame: University of Notre Dame Press, 1974.

Schmitter, Philippe C., and Gerhard Lehmbruch, eds. *Trends Toward Corporatist Intermediation.* Beverly Hills: Sage, 1979.

Schneider, Ronald M. *The Political System of Brazil: Emergence of a*

"Modernizing" Authoritarian Regime, 1964–1970. New York: Columbia University Press, 1971.

Schwartzman, Simon. "Back to Weber: Corporatism and Patrimonialism in the Seventies." In *Authoritarianism and Corporatism in Latin America*, ed. J. M. Malloy. Pittsburgh: University of Pittsburgh Press, 1977.

———. *Bases do Autoritarismo Brasileiro*. Rio de Janeiro: Editora Campus, 1982.

Seeman Melvin. "Alienation and Social Learning in a Reformatory." *American Journal of Sociology* 69 (1963): 270–84.

———. "Alienation, Membership, and Political Knowledge: A Comparative Study." *Public Opinion Quarterly* 30 (1966): 353–67.

———. "On the Meaning of Alienation." *American Sociological Review* 24 (1959): 783–91.

Seeman, Melvin, and John W. Evans. "Alienation and Learning in a Hospital Setting." *American Sociological Review* 27 (1962): 772–82.

Serra, José. "Three Mistaken Theses Regarding the Connection between Industrialization and Authoritarian Regimes." In *The New Authoritarianism in Latin America*, ed. David Collier. Princeton: Princeton University Press, 1979.

Sheahan, John. "Market-Oriented Economic Policies and Political Repression in Latin America." *Economic Development and Cultural Change* (1980): 264–89.

Shefter, Martin. "Trade Unions and Political Machines: The Organization and Disorganization of the American Working Class in the Late Nineteenth Century." In *Working Class Formation: Nineteenth Century Patterns in Western Europe and the United States*, ed. Ira Katznelson and Aristide Zolberg. Princeton: Princeton University Press, 1986.

Simão, Azis. *Sindicato e Estado*. São Paulo: Atica, 1981.

Simon, Herbert. "Causation." In *The International Encyclopedia of the Social Sciences*. New York: Macmillan, 1968.

———. Models of Man. New York: Wiley, 1957.

Simon, Herbert, and N. Rescher. "Cause and Counterfactual." *Philosophy of Science* 33:324–40.

Simonsen, Mário H. *Brasil 2001*. Rio de Janeiro: Apec, 1979.

Simonsen, Mário H., and Roberto de O. Campos. *A Nova Economia Brasileira*. Rio de Janeiro: José Olympio, 1974.

Singer, Paul. *A Crise do Milagre: Interpretação Crítica da Economia Brasileira*. Rio de Janeiro: Paz e Terra, 1977.

Skidmore, Thomas E. "Politics and Economic Policy Making in Authoritarian Brazil, 1937–71." In *Authoritarian Brazil,* ed. Alfred Stepan. New Haven: Yale University Press, 1973.

———. *Politics in Brazil.* London: Oxford University Press, 1967.

———. "The Politics of Economic Stabilization in Post War Latin America." In *Authoritarianism and Corporatism in Latin America,* ed. J. M. Malloy. Pittsburgh: University of Pittsburgh Press, 1977.

Skocpol, Theda. "Bringing the State Back In: Strategies of Analysis in Current Research." In *Bringing the State Back In,* ed. Peter B. Evans, D. Rueschemeyer, and Theda Skocpol. Cambridge: Cambridge University Press, 1985.

———. *States and Social Revolutions: A Comparative Analysis of France, Russia, and China.* Cambridge: Cambridge University Press, 1979.

Skowroneck, Stephen. *Building a New American State: The Expansion of National Administrative Capacities.* Cambridge: Cambridge University Press, 1982.

Soares, G. A. Dillon. *Sociedade e Política no Brasil.* São Paulo: Difel, 1973.

Souza, Amaury de. "The Nature of Corporative Representation: Leaders and Members of Organized Labor in Brazil." Ph.D. diss., Massachusetts Institute of Technology, 1978.

Souza, Amaury de, and Bolivar Lamounier. "Governo e Sindicatos no Brasil: A Perspectiva dos Anos 80." *Dados* 24 (1981): 139–59.

Souza, Maria do Carmo Campello de. *Estado e Partidos Políticos no Brasil (1930 a 1964).* São Paulo: Alfa-Ômega, 1976.

Souza Martins, Heloisa Helena Teixeira de. *O Estado e a Burocratização do Sindicato no Brasil.* São Paulo: Hucitec, 1979.

Souza Warhlich, Beatriz M. de. *Reforma Administrativa na Era de Vargas.* Rio de Janeiro: FGV, 1968.

Stepan, Alfred, ed. *Authoritarian Brazil.* New Haven: Yale University Press, 1973.

———. *The Military in Politics: Changing Patterns in Brazil.* Princeton: Princeton University Press, 1971.

———. "Political Leadership and Regime Breakdown: Brazil." In *The Breakdown of Democratic Regimes,* ed. Juan J. Linz and Alfred Stepan. Baltimore: Johns Hopkins University Press, 1978.

———. "State Power and the Strength of Civil Society in the Southern Cone of Latin America." In *Bringing the State Back In,* ed. Peter Evans, D. Rueschemeyer, and T. Skocpol. Cambridge: Cambridge University Press, 1985.

———. *The State and Society: Peru in Comparative Perspective*. Princeton: Princeton University Press, 1978.

Stinchcombe, A. *Constructing Social Theories*. New York: Harcourt, Brace and World, 1968.

Stumpf, André G., and Merval P. Filho. *A Segunda Guerra: Sucessão de Geisel*. São Paulo: Editora Brasiliense, 1979.

Supple, Barry. "The State and the Industrial Revolution 1700–1914." In *The Fontana Economic History of Europe*, vol. 3, ed. Carlo M. Cipolla. London: Collins/Fontana Books, 1973.

Tedeschi, James T., and Thomas V. Bonoma. "Power and Influence: An Introduction." In *The Social Influence Processes*, ed. James T. Tedeschi. Chicago: Aldine-Atherton, 1972.

Tilly, Charles, ed. *The Formation of National States in Western Europe*. Princeton: Princeton University Press, 1975.

Tolipan, Ricardo and A. C. Tinelli, eds. *A Controvérsia Sobre Distribuição de Renda e Desenvolvimento*. Rio de Janeiro: Zahar, 1975.

Touraine, Alain. "Industrialization et Conscience Ouvrière à São Paulo." *Sociologie du Travail* 4 (1961): 77–95.

Trimberger, Ellen K. *Revolution from Above: Military Bureaucrats and Development in Japan, Turkey, Egypt and Peru*. New Brunswick: Transaction Books, 1978.

Tronca, Italo. "O Exército e a Industrialização Entre as Armas e Volta Redonda (1930–1942)." In *História Geral da Civilização Brasileira*. (Tomo 3, vol. 3. São Paulo: Difel, 1981.

Uricochea, Fernando. *The Patrimonial Foundations of the Brazilian Bureaucratic State*. Berkeley and Los Angeles: University of California Press, 1980.

Valenzuela, Julio S. "The Chilean Labor Movement: The Institutionalization of Conflict." In *Chile: Politics and Society*, ed. A. Valenzuela and J. S. Valenzuela. New Brunswick: Transaction Books, 1976.

Vargas, Getúlio. *A Nova Política do Brasil*. Vol. 1. Rio de Janeiro: José Olympio, 1938.

Veliz, Claudio. *The Centralist Tradition of Latin America*. Princeton: Princeton University Press, 1980.

Verba, Sidney, and Norman H. Nie. *Participation in America: Political Democracy and Social Equality*. New York: Harper & Row, 1972.

Vianna, Luiz Werneck. "Estudos Sobre Sindicalismo e Movimento Operário: Resenha de Algumas Tendências." *Dados* 17 (1978): 9–24.

———. *Liberalismo e Sindicato no Brasil.* Rio de Janeiro: Paz e Terra, 1978.

Vieira, Evaldo. *Autoritarismo e Corporativismo no Brasil.* São Paulo: Cortez Editora, 1981.

Villela, Anibal, and Wilson Suzigan. *Política do Govêrno e Crescimento da Economia Brasileira, 1889–1945.* Rio de Janeiro: IPEA/INPES, 1973.

Wall, Grenville. "The Concept of Interest in Politics." *Politics and Society* 5 (1975); 487–510.

Wallerstein, Immanuel. *The Modern World System: Capitalist Agriculture and the Origins of the European World-Economy in the Sixteenth Century.* New York: Academic Press, 1974.

Wallerstein, Michael. "The Collapse of Democracy in Brazil." *Latin American Research Review* (1980): 3–49.

Weber, Max. *The Theory of Social and Economic Organization,* ed. Talcott Parsons. New York: Free Press, 1947.

Weffort, Francisco C. "Origens do Sindicalismo Populista no Brasil: A Conjuntura do Após-Guerra." *Estudos CEBRAP* (1973): 65–105.

———. *Participação e Conflito Industrial: Contagem e Osasco 1968.* Cadernos CEBRAP 5. São Paulo: CEBRAP, 1972.

———. *O Populismo na Política Brasileira.* Rio de Janeiro: Paz e Terra, 1980.

———. "Sindicatos e Política." Ph.D. diss., University of São Paulo, 1972.

———. "State and Mass in Brazil." In *Masses in Latin America,* ed. Irving L. Horowitz. New York: Oxford University Press, 1971.

Weissberg, Robert. *Political Learning, Political Choice, and Democratic Citizeship.* Englewood Cliffs: Prentice-Hall, 1974.

Wiarda, Howard J. "Corporatism and Development in the Iberic-Latin World: Persistent Strains and New Variations." In *The New Corporatism,* ed. F. B. Pike and T. Stritch. Notre Dame: University of Notre Dame Press, 1974.

Winkler, J. T. "Corporatism." *Archives Européenes de Sociologie* (1976): 100–36.

Wirth, John D. *The Politics of Brazilian Development.* Stanford: Stanford University Press, 1970.

Wolff, Robert Paul. *The Poverty of Liberalism.* Boston: Beacon, 1968.

Wolfinger, Raymond E. "Nondecisions and the Study of Local Politics." *American Political Science Review* 65 (1971): 1063–80.

Wrong, Dennis H. *Power: Its Forms, Bases and Uses.* New York: Harper, 1979.

Index

Pitt Latin American Series

COLE BLASIER, EDITOR

ARGENTINA

Argentina in the Twentieth Century
David Rock, Editor

Argentina: Political Culture and Instability
Susan Calvert and Peter Calvert

Discreet Partners: Argentina and the USSR Since 1917
Aldo César Vacs

Juan Perón and the Reshaping of Argentina
Frederick C. Turner and José Enrique Miguens, Editors

The Life, Music, and Times of Carlos Gardel
Simon Collier

The Political Economy of Argentina, 1946–1983
Guido di Tella and Rudiger Dornbusch, Editors

BRAZIL

External Constraints on Economic Policy in Brazil, 1899–1930
Winston Fritsch

The Film Industry in Brazil: Culture and the State
Randal Johnson

Manipulation of Consent: The State and Working-Class Consciousness in Brazil
Youssef Cohen

The Politics of Social Security in Brazil
James M. Malloy

Urban Politics in Brazil: The Rise of Populism, 1925–1945
Michael L. Conniff

COLOMBIA

Gaitán of Colombia: A Political Biography
Richard E. Sharpless

Roads to Reason: Transportation, Administration, and Rationality in Colombia
Richard E. Hartwig

CUBA

Cuba Between Empires, 1878–1902
Louis A. Pérez, Jr.

Cuba, Castro, and the United States
Philip W. Bonsal

Cuba in the World
Cole Blasier and Carmelo Mesa-Lago, Editors

Cuba Under the Platt Amendment
Louis A. Pérez, Jr.

Cuban Studies, Vols. 16–19
Carmelo Mesa-Lago, Editor

Intervention, Revolution, and Politics in Cuba, 1913–1921
Louis A. Pérez, Jr.

Lords of the Mountain: Social Banditry and Peasant Protest in Cuba, 1878–1918
Louis A. Pérez, Jr.

Revolutionary Change in Cuba
Carmelo Mesa-Lago, Editor

The United States and Cuba: Hegemony and Dependent Development, 1880–1934
Jules Robert Benjamin

MEXICO

The Mexican Republic: The First Decade, 1823–1832
Stanley C. Green

Mexico Through Russian Eyes, 1806–1940
William Harrison Richardson

Oil and Mexican Foreign Policy
George W. Grayson

The Politics of Mexican Oil
George W. Grayson

Voices, Visions and a New Reality: Mexican Fiction Since 1970
J. Ann Duncan

US POLICIES

Cuba, Castro, and the United States
Philip W. Bonsal

The Hovering Giant: U.S. Responses to Revolutionary Change in Latin America
Cole Blasier

Illusions of Conflict: Anglo-American Diplomacy Toward Latin America
Joseph Smith

The United States and Cuba: Hegemony and Dependent Development, 1880–1934
Jules Robert Benjamin

The United States and Latin America in the 1980s: Contending Perspectives on a Decade of Crisis
Kevin J. Middlebrook and Carlos Rico, Editors

USSR POLICIES

Discreet Partners: Argentina and the USSR Since 1917
Aldo César Vacs

The Giant's Rival: The USSR and Latin America
Cole Blasier

Mexico Through Russian Eyes, 1806–1940
William Harrison Richardson

OTHER NATIONAL STUDIES

Beyond the Revolution: Bolivia Since 1952
James M. Malloy and Richard S. Thorn, Editors

Black Labor on a White Canal: Panama, 1904–1981
Michael L. Conniff

The Catholic Church and Politics in Nicaragua and Costa Rica
Philip J. Williams

The Origins of the Peruvian Labor Movement, 1883–1919
Peter Blanchard

The Overthrow of Allende and the Politics of Chile, 1964–1976
Paul E. Sigmund

Panajachel: A Guatemalan Town in Thirty-Year Perspective
Robert E. Hinshaw

Peru and the International Monetary Fund
Thomas Scheetz

Primary Medical Care in Chile: Accessibility Under Military Rule
Joseph L. Scarpaci

Rebirth of the Paraguayan Republic: The First Colorado Era, 1878–1904
Harris G. Warren

Restructuring Domination: Industrialists and the State in Ecuador
Catherine M. Conaghan

SOCIAL SECURITY

The Politics of Social Security in Brazil
James M. Malloy

Social Security in Latin America: Pressure Groups, Stratification, and Inequality
Carmelo Mesa-Lago

OTHER STUDIES

Adventurers and Proletarians: The Story of Migrants in Latin America
Magnus Mörner, with the collaboration of Harold Sims

Authoritarianism and Corporatism in Latin America
James M. Malloy, Editor

Authoritarianism and Democrats: Regime Transition in Latin America
James M. Malloy and Mitchell. A Seligson, Editors

The Catholic Church and Politics in Nicaragua and Costa Rica
Philip J. Williams

Female and Male in Latin America: Essays
Ann Pescatello, Editor

Latin American Debt and the Adjustment Crisis
Rosemary Thorp and Laurence Whitehead, Editors

Public Policy in Latin America: A Comparative Survey
John W. Sloan

Selected Latin American One-Act Plays
Francesca Collecchia and Julio Matas, Editors and Translators

The State and Capital Accumulation in Latin America: Brazil, Chile, Mexico
Christian Anglade and Carlos Fortin, Editors

Transnational Corporations and the Latin American Automobile Industry
Rhys Jenkins